A Treasury of Hunting and Fishing Humor

Edited by
James E. Myers

THE LINCOLN-HERNDON PRESS, INC.
818 South Dirksen Parkway
Springfield, Illinois 62703

Published by Lincoln-Herndon Press, Inc.
818 South Dirksen Parkway
Springfield, Illinois 62703
217-522-2732

Printed in the United States of America

Library of Congress Cataloging-in-Publication Data

ISBN 0-942936-19-1: $10.95
Library of Congress Catalogue Card Number 90-063400
Fourth Printing

Cover illustration by
Richard Ferguson
Squires Advertising Agency, Inc.
Springfield, Illinois

Typography by
Mark Ritterbusch
Communication Design
Rochester, Illinois

FISHING
SECTION

"Oh yeah, Charlie — I forgot to tell you to watch for holes out here."

Behold the fisherman!
He riseth early in the morning
and disturbeth
The whole household.
Mighty are his prospects.
He goeth forth full of hope,
and when the day
Is far spent he returneth — smelling of
Strong drink; and the truth
is not in him.

INTRODUCTION

To begin it all...we'll start with fishing stories (hunting stories begin on page 112) and with President Herbert Hoover (1929-1933) who offers us some wonderful material to begin with. He was a devoted fisherman, "an outdoorsman." His little book, FISHIN' FOR FUN — AND TO WASH YOUR SOUL is unparalleled in its description of the fun and "soul-washing" that fishermen experience.

And fishing IS fun. It offers opportunity to pal around with other like-minded folks — fishergals and fisherguys who are always your friends (unless you try to take over the territory in which they're fishing). No fisherperson (no sexist comments, please) ever went to the jailhouse for fishing — unless, of course, he forgot to buy a license.

Further, as President Hoover tells us, "fishing reduces the ego in presidents and former presidents for at fishing most men are not equal to boys."

The President goes on to comment, "A good fisherman possesses much faith and hope or he would not fish. He gains even in charity when he listens to other fishermen."

The President tells this cute story. He was returning from a day's fishing and he had caught no fish, was absolutely skunked. He happened to meet a boy who was carrying a wonderful string of fish. President Hoover asked, "And just where did you catch all those fish, young fellow?"

The kid replied, "You go down that lane where it says 'PRIVATE' till you come up to a sign that says 'Trespassers Will Be Prosecuted'. Now, you go on just a leetle further to a stream where a sign says 'No Fishing Allowed.' You stop, get out your rod and fish right there 'cause that's where I caught these fish."

In his superb book, STORIES OF THE OLD DUCK HUNTERS & OTHER DRIVEL, Gordon MacQuarrie has this to say about the tendency of fishermen to slightly exaggerate...a teenie-weenie bit — when they honestly describe a fish they caught — (or almost caught).

> *"You are an unregenerate back-slider," said I to the president of the Old Duck Hunters' Association, Inc.*
> *"You bet your life I am," he answered spiritedly.*
> *"You are," I went on, "a hypocritical rascal without principle or virtue of any kind of your mangy hide."*
> *"Right again," agreed the president.*
> *"This water is perfect for a dry fly and I'll stake my reputation on it."*
> *"Your reputation!" The woods rang with his laughter. "Shucks, sonny, you ain't got no reputation. You're a fisherman."*

Now the reader must remember that this canard, this unjust criticism, this unjustified malignment of truth-telling fishermen was done by a hunter. Wouldn't you know! So let us forget his incautious remark and admit that, rarely, if ever, do fishermen exaggerate...just the slightest bit. But even the angels do that. So what's the harm? There is none; that's what!

But, lest we do him an injustice, there is a quiet, reflective side to Mr. MacQuarrie as he writes about the inner peace, the expansion of the soul, that fishermen experience at their holy game: "You are as relaxed physically and mentally as you will ever be. The river has reached out like an old friend and made a place for you."

Poetic? Lyrical? True? You bet. But there is still another side to the man, and without the grin!

"Unlike poker, golf or bowling, if you aren't cautious, that river, the outdoors, can kill you. Nature, out there, can be plumb dangerous. She can kill you dead in the water if you are stupid, unlucky or ignorant of how to get along with her. But the element of danger adds zip, gusto, zest — salt and pepper — the stimulation we all need and that fishermen find in fishing.

There's a story that illustrates this "I'll do it or else" attitude of the committed fisherman.

It seems that an old man, a fisherman since boyhood, was told that he should prepare himself for the day when the old bearded gent with the big, sharp sickle would come and substitute heaven, the hereafter, for this good earth.

"Let the old bastard come," the old man said, "but he's got to guarantee that they got trout, bass and pike fishin' up there. He'd damned well better be prepared to gar-r-r-antee they got fishin' up there."

"Wait a cotton-pickin' minute, old fellow," his young friend responded. "You know you can't dictate terms to that old sickle-chopper gent. He isn't going to dicker or deal with you!"

"In that case," growled the old fisherman, "I ain't goin."

It's a cute story and most devoted, experienced and able fishermen fit that pattern. Such a man has the gutsy, defiant, go-to-hell quality about him that goes to make the man he is. And long may he be...with his casting rod, his fly-rod, his worms or flies or plugs or minnies. And may he never quit telling stories (mixed with a few whoppers and windies) as good or better than the stories you are about to read. Think of them when it pours down rain on you, when the midges eat on your hide, when you get over your boots in water, and when you come home empty-creeled. Wash your soul with fishing, as President Hoover advised, and bathe your spirit with laughter. It's still the best medicine.

This could be the fish that prompted the observer to say: "The man who caught that fish is a liar!" But this is the honest-to-Gawd, s'help me, everlastin' true photo of a buffalo fish caught near St. Louis, Missouri in 1920. This photo is reproduced with permission of the Missouri Historical Society

Many Americans do not know that our former President of the United States, Herbert Hoover, was an enthusiastic, capable and philosophical fisherman. In his precious book about his views and ways of fishing, *Fishing For Fun And To Wash Your Soul,* he offered this advice on the wisdom of stuffing and displaying fish.

ON STUFFING FISH FOR HOUSEHOLD ORNAMENTS — FOR PROOF OF PROWESS

On those rare occasions during deep-sea fishing when you get a monster on board, your first thought is to perpetuate your triumph and convince your wife you caught him. The first step to evidence is to have him weighed by the wharfkeeper and get a written certificate. It is useful to give the wharfkeeper a tip. The second step of evidence for your wife is to have him stuffed. This is also the way to demonstrate to all persons your great triumph. That costs $175 per fish, paid in advance.

After he is stuffed and you have paid the bill and the freight and truck charges, you must mount him over the living-room mantel, where you hope he will provide a conversational item, and that all your guests will marvel. You can gently blend in your great skill, courage and endurance. The neighbors only come once.

By and by your wife disapproves of him as a household ornament and insists he has moths. Anyway, she bribes the garbage man with five dollars to take him away while you are at the office.

If you are inclined toward having your fish stuffed, I suggest you wait until you can observe the rubbish barges going to the dump at sea. You can see them in the early morning at the piers. And you will find them topped with stuffed fish. The barge man will accommodate you with one for a dollar or less — and throw in for free the moths and weevils.

✻   ✻   ✻   ✻

It is appropriate that we offer this collection of fish stories with the first fish story of all...that of old man Noah and his Ark. Also appropriate is it that the tale is by an Englishman whose land is surrounded by water and fish, hence, bound to be authentic. So here is S. John Peskett's Noah story as published by Thorton Butterworth, Ltd. London.

IN THE BEGINNING

'And in that Heaven of all their wish,
There shall be no more land, say fish.'

The fishes' Heaven was realized long, long ago at the time of the Flood. In fact the Flood was a busman's holiday for the fishes. As the waters rose over the habitations of sinful mankind, they found their territories immeasurably increased and they saw things no fishy eye had ever seen before.

It was the happy fate of the fish world to be preserved, although only two specimens each of every other form of life, apart from the nautical Noahs, were permitted to escape destruction. Possibly it was ordained that the fishes should have their Heaven at the beginning of time instead of having it at the tailend like us. This raises the rather interesting point that it will possibly not be necessary to have water in Heaven, apart from the small quantity which Lazarus might have in hand to taunt Dives from the comfortable security of Abraham's bosom. There will certainly be no need of water for washing or any other practical purpose, and if there should be any need of beverages, we might reasonably expect something with more spirit in it. It is therefore quite possible that there was some purpose in giving the fishes their Heaven when water was plentiful and thus saving the necessity of providing for them later on.

An alternative reason for the preservation of the fish world is that it would have increased Noah's difficulties considerably to have had to take into the Ark large numbers of glass bowls with two fishes in each. One problem in particular would have presented itself: could one pair of ants and one pair of worms have produced sufficient ant eggs and little worms to feed the fish population of the Ark for any period? Moreover, the whales would have caused quite a lot of trouble, even if the Ark could have been enlarged beyond the prescribed dimensions to accommodate them. Even if two whales were taken in tow, it would have been found very difficult to steer the Ark with any degree of accuracy and we have no evidence for supposing that Noah had any previous nautical training. So perhaps everything was for the best. We are thus able to present the fish world in the heyday of its history.

When the last fowl of the air and the last beast of the field had been gathered into the Ark, the hatches were battened down, the anchor was drawn up and the good ship was soon under way, destination unknown. But down in the watery depths, the fishes were beginning to realize that they were on the brink of a great adventure. They saw their domains extend on every side and it is at this point that the history of the fish world begins.

'Two of each kind'

The Sea: The fisherman's farm.

* * * *

Here is an insight into the soul of the fisherman as given us in yet another look at THE BOOK OF JONAH. This gem was related by Walt Mason in 1916 in a lovely little book entitled HIS BOOK. The introduction was written by a great and sensible fisherman and humorist whom many readers will know, Irvin Cobb. Please note that the conclusion of this story/tale will seem eminently sensible to most fishermen.

Once a fisherman was dying in his humble, lowly cot, and the pastor sat beside him saying things that hit the spot, so that all his futile terrors left the dying sinner's heart, and he said: "The journey's lonely, but I'm ready for the start. There is just one little matter that is fretting me," he sighed, "and perhaps I'd better tell it ere I cross the Great Divide. I have got a string of stories that I've told from day to day; stories of the fish I've captured, and the ones that got away, and I fear that when I tell them they are apt to stretch a mile. And I wonder when I'm wafted to that land that's free from guile, if they'll let me tell my stories if I try to tell them straight, or will angels lose their tempers then, and chase me through the gate?" Then the pastor sat and pondered, for the question vexed him sore; never such a weird conundrum had been sprung on him before. Yet the courage of conviction moved him soon to reply, and he wished to fill the fisher with fair visions of the sky: "You can doubtless tell fish stories," said the clergyman, aloud, "but I'd stretch them very little if old Jonah's in the crowd."

And while we are concerned with these biblical characters, let us consider the wisdom of a contemporary preacher and his approach to the squeaky matter of Sunday fishing.

The Reverend Malchizadek Jones was not only a good preacher but a good and pious man. Too, there was a strong streak of the practical in him.

On a Sunday evening, Pooter Elder, a member of Reverend Jones's congregation, presented the pastor with a string of first-rate bass.

"But I must tell you, Pastor Jones, 'cause you got a right to know. Them there fish was caught on Sunday."

"Pooter, I sure do thank you for thinking of me. Now...my first thought about these Sunday-caught fish is to give them back to you. But...well...hm-m-m...my second thought tells me that the Lord knows and you know and I know...that these here bass were not to blame."

"GUESS WHAT JUST GOT AWAY!"

Fishing: A jerk at one end of the line waiting for a jerk at the other end. (A wisecrack by a non-fisherman, of course).

* * * *

Two priests were taken by a friend to the Superior National Forest for their first fishing experience. On the first day, the guide described Father O'Brien's Walleye Pike as "a big sonovabitch!" And Father O'Brien, of course, and quite naturally, thought that was the name of the fish. A bit later, Father Garvey caught a small Great Northern Pike that the guide described as "a little bastard." And so it went throughout the three-day trip.

Back home for their first meal of the fish they had caught, they were joined by a new priest, freshly ordained and black, named Father Jefferson.

At table, Father O'Brien asked to have passed "a piece of that Big Sonovabitch." Then Father Garvey said "I believe I'll have a bit of 'The Little Bastard.'"

The new and bemused Father Jefferson remarked, "WOW! I'm sure goin' to like this mutha-fuckin' place."

* * * *

Fisherman: A delusion entirely surrounded by liars in old clothes.

* * * *

It was a fruitless day for a certain fisherman fishing on the Lake of the Woods. Then he saw another boat loaded with fish. "What you using for bait?" he called out.

"I'm a physician-surgeon," the successful fisherman replied. "And I save all tonsils I remove and use 'em for bait. They make the best bait of all."

"I'm no physician, but please tell me where you caught 'em and I'll try there." He was told, then rowed to the spot, but caught nothing.

Soon he was passed by another boat, simply loaded to the gunwales with fish. "What you using for bait?" he called out to the lucky fisherman.

"I'm a veterinarian," the other replied. "When I castrate pigs, I save the balls. They make swell bait."

"I'm no vet," said the unlucky fisherman, "but if you'd be so good as to tell me where you caught 'em, I'd sure like to try there." He's given directions, then rows to the spot. But he doesn't get so much as a nibble.

He works away until another boat comes by. It, too, is loaded with fish. "Say, mister, what you using for bait?" Our luckless fisherman asked the bearded occupant of the other boat. "Well, I'm a rabbi, you see, and...."

* * * *

He lies like a rug: The average fisherman.

* * * *

The County Farm Advisor was discussing with a farmer the poor showing he had made from his farm the last few years. "George, you've got a mighty fine spread of land here, and you could make good money if you'd just spend more time farming this place and less time fishing down at your pond."

"Could be," the farmer replied, "but I want you to take a good look at this map of the world. Why, this earth is two-thirds water and one-third land. Now, that suggests to me that to be in touch with the way things are, a man is supposed to fish two-thirds of the time and farm one-third."

* * * *

Irvin S. Cobb, an early humorist and keen fisherman, told of his passing an old tenant house after a downpour of rain. He knew the tenant and stopped to chat. After a bit of conversation, he cleared his throat and asked the old boy why he sat in front of his door, holding a fishing rod with the line out in a big puddle in front of the house. "Sam, you old fool, how come you're trying to fish in a silly old mud puddle like that?"

"Well, hmmm, y'see..."

"Now you know as well as I do that there ain't any fish there."

"Yeah. Sure I do. But it's jest so danged handy here, is all...."

" MARTHA, DON'T YOU SEE MY LINE IS BUSY ?"

A fisherman was describing a fish he had caught. He held his hands wide apart, about as far as his arms could stretch, and said, "It was this long, man. Why I never saw sech a fish!"

"I sure can believe that!" his friend replied.

*   *   *   *

And then there's the story of a man gazing at a huge, enormous mounted bass. He shook his head in disbelief, then remarked, "The man who caught that there fish is a liar!"

One of the all-time great fish stories goes like this: Two fishermen were discussing their experiences during the previous day's catch. One fellow said he'd caught a salmon that weighed 200 pounds.

"Two hundred pounds!" exclaimed the other man. "Why, you and I both know that no salmon gets that big."

"That's what you say. But mine weighed that much. Now tell me.. what did you catch?"

"Had a poor day. Hooked me a rusty old lamp that had incised on the bottom: 'Property of Christopher Columbus, 1492.' And you know, the oddest thing was, that there was a candle inside and that derned old candle was still lit!"

"Tell you what," said the salmon fisherman. "You blow out that damned candle, and I'll knock off one hundred and fifty pounds."

* * * *

Fish hooks: No, not the curved, barbed kind...merely the fingers.

"STOP GRUMBLING! YOU'LL MEET FRIENDS YOU HAVEN'T SEEN SINCE NURSERY SCHOOL!"

It was not the season for black bass, but Eddie Jones had caught a dandy. Unfortunately, the game warden discovered his fish and announced, "That fish is going to cost you $25, sir, because it is out-of-season for bass."

"Beg pardon, warden, but I never break the law. Let me tell you what happened. That damned black bass was eating the bait off my hook faster than I could put it on. Now, warden, you wouldn't expect me to come way out here and submit to that, would you? So I just tied him up here out of harms way so I could get on with my fishing. And that's the truth!"

* * * *

The young boy was late for Sunday School, and his teacher asked him why he was tardy. The kid hemmed and hawed a bit and then said, "I was all set to go fishing, and then my daddy stopped me."

The teacher smiled, nodded and said, "Your daddy is a good man. He is bringing you up in the right way, never to violate the Sabbath, even to go fishing. Did your daddy explain to you why?"

"Oh yes. Sure did. He pointed out that there simply wasn't enough bait for the two of us, so one had to stay home. That's me."

* * * *

Fish-wrapper: Newspaper.

* * * *

Eddie Smart was walking along the bank of Lake Springfield when he passed a dozing fisherman.

"There's a nibble on your line, man," Eddie said, nudging the man.

"By gosh, you're right. Much obliged. Now, sir, would you mind reeling in the line for me?"

Eddie obliged the fellow and landed a good bass, then turned to leave.

"Sure thank you," the man said, "but would you do me a favor and take him off the hook?"

So Eddie turned and removed the fish, "And now I'd suspect you want me to bait the hook?" Eddie asked sarcastically.

"Well...that sure would be nice of you, sir..."

So Eddie began to bait the hook, saying, "You're the laziest man I've seen in a long time. You really ought to get married so's to have a kid of your own who could go fishin' with you and pull in the fish and bait your hook."

"By golly, you're right!" the man said with his first sign of enthusiasm. "Do you know where I could find me a pregnant woman?"

* * * *

Teacher: Now class, can any of you tell me what a fish net is made of?

Eight year old: A whole lot of little holes tied together with string.

* * * *

First pelican: "Wow! That's a mighty fine fish you got there."

Second pelican: "Not bad. It fills the bill."

Upstream, Downstream and Out of My Mind. Syd Hoff. © 1961

An old man sat on the bank of the river watching his bobber move slowly along. He had jumped the gun as it was a week before fishing season would open. A game warden came up behind him and watched him for a few minutes, then said: "You fishin', old man?"

The old man looked up, then waggled his pole a bit, then lifted his line out of the water to reveal a minnow wriggling on the end of his line. "Me? Fishin'? Hell no. I'm jest teachin' this here minnie how to swim!"

* * * *

Like the boy the cat ran over: speechless. The way a fisherman felt when his buddy bragged about a 10" bass he'd caught. "A 10-inch bass? That's not so big."

"Oh yes it is! That's 10 inches from eye to eye!"

* * * *

Some of the best fishermen got married because a woman bit on their line.

* * * *

Wife: "How many fish did you tell me you caught last Saturday?"

Hubby: "Six, honey, and were they beauties."

Wife: "Well, that dadblamed fish department at the store made a mistake again. They charged us for eight!"

* * * *

Fish horn: A saxophone.

* * * *

"Women sure are strange," the town philosopher-fisherman said. "They complain like crazy about the man they caught and only brag about the ones that got away."

* * * *

Then there's the story of the wife out fishing with her husband. She turns to him and asks, "Have you another cork, dear? This one simply won't stay afloat."

They say, and it's true, "Friends, Fishing and Fresh Garden Sass are just about all that goes to make life worth living."

* * * *

The old-timer said, "For fight, fun, stamina and tricks, I'll take a small-mouth lass at sundown any old time."

* * * *

A New England fisherman watched an outlandishly dressed visitor waltz down the street of a seaside resort town. The fisherman turned to his buddy and remarked, "I reckon the riggin's wuth more'n the hull."

* * * *

Caterpillar: A critter with wormlike appearance that can be used as bait. It is found on grass, twigs, flowers, under rocks, etc. But it is most readily found on the back of a fisherman's neck!

* * * *

When a man moves into a situation he'd better avoid, some say, "He's fixin' to plow up snakes." Others say, "He's stirrin' up yellow jackets in the shit house." But a true fisherman would say, in masterful understatement, "He's fishin' in troubled waters."

* * * *

Ethnic groups take their licks at various times — Polish, Scotch, English, Jewish, and here is one about the Irish. It seems that two Americans were fishing on the Connemara River. A local passed by, put a worm on his hook and within a minute or two caught a seven-pound salmon. The American watched in surprise, then confusion, as the man measured the fish then threw it back in the river and began to bait his hook again.

"Hey, buddy, we don't mind you bustin' in on our fishing area, but just why in the hell did you throw that good fish back?"

"Arrah," said the Irisher, "bless you in your innocence, you nice Americans. But, you see, my pan is only six inches wide."

* * * *

You might call the following statement, a defense of women.

Man complains much about women but we know there are at least four things in her favor:

Number one: She never pays $50 boat rent to get where the fish aren't.

Number two: She never enters a restaurant to order a $10 meal, then tips the pretty waitress $4 because she smiled at her.

Number three: She doesn't waste $8 on a box of shotgun shells to kill a rabbit she could buy at the store for $4.

Number four: She doesn't spend $150 on a fly-fishing rod to catch a trout that the store sells for $5.

* * * *

Smelt: A highly edible fish, truly delicious, that should go to court and get its name changed.

* * * *

Nothing grows faster than a fish between the time the fish takes the bait...and the time he gets away.

* * * *

You surely won't believe me,
I was fishing yesterday.
And the fish I got was bigger
Than the fish that got away.

* * * *

An arrival at the Pearly Gates was met by St. Peter who said, "Tough luck, fellow, but you told too many lies while you lived on earth. You aren't coming in here."

"Hey, St. Peter! Aren't you forgetting something? Now put on your thinkin' cap. Remember when you, too, were a fisherman?"

"Something's come up and I can't go fishing with you fellows."

Upstream, Downstream and Out of My Mind. Syd Hoff. © 1961

A New Yorker was visiting at a lake in Wisconsin. He asked an old fellow, who was fishing from the dock, if fishing had been good.

"You bet!"

"What kind have you been catching?"

"Bass, Walleyes, Great Northerns...every kind that's up here."

"What is the biggest fish you ever pulled out of this lake?"

"Well, mister, I never weighed it. But I'm an honest guy, and so I simply won't estimate how much that bugger weighed. But I can tell you this...when I pulled it out of the lake, the water level went down three feet."

Crappie: Like the smelt, a mighty-good-eatin' fish. But it, too, should go have its name changed.

* * * *

Mal de Mer: Caused by very rough water. Translation: You can't take it with you.

* * * *

They say that fishing is extra good during the tourist season down in Florida. The reason is that the bikinis are so sexy the tide refuses to go out.

* * * *

It got so dry in Vermont, back in the thirties, that there were trout three years old that had never learned how to swim.

* * * *

A fisherman was bragging about a 15-pound salmon he had landed.

"Fifteen pounds!" exclaimed the other. "Did you have witnesses?"

"Sure did. Otherwise it would have weighed twenty-five pounds."

* * * *

The village parson was taking a walk through the woods when he came upon Jeff Tonker, a parishioner of his, fishing in a lovely stream. "Jeff!" exclaimed the parson, "Why are you fishing when your wife is home working — cleaning, cooking, preparing for the church supper! Why aren't you home helping her?"

"Well, Parson, suh, it's like this...there ain't no use my bein' there. She'll work jest as hard as if I was there keepin' track of things !"

* * * *

Do like they do in Alabama. What you do when it's time for supper and you've caught no fish. Do without!

Preacher: "Can you tell me one of the parables, my child?"

Eddie: "I think I can."

Preacher: "Then by all means let me hear it."

Eddie: "I know the one about the feller who loafs and fishes."

✳   ✳   ✳   ✳

It is mighty hard to outdo a fisherman. At Lake Springfield, an avid angler pulled up to the dock with a string of a dozen crappie, all about the size of sardines. He was joined by another fellow who proudly laid down beside the string of crappie, his catch, a single catfish about 4 feet long, weighing about 24-pounds. Not to be outdone, our avid crappie angler took a long look at the big fish and then remarked: "Hmmm. Too bad. Just caught the one, eh?"

✳   ✳   ✳   ✳

Fish or cut bait: Get to it, do it or let someone else try! A common phrase every American understands.

✳   ✳   ✳   ✳

One of those do-gooders with an artificial bleeding heart remarked to a fisherman, "It's shameful! A big man like you ought to be able to better occupy himself than catching those poor little fish!"

But the fisherman had the right reply. "Ma'am, you'll pardon me for saying this, but, if that there fish had just kept his big mouth shut...he never would have been caught."

✳   ✳   ✳   ✳

Fish: A newcomer or novice. Also, a dollar bill.

An old black man was quietly fishing from the banks of a well known trout stream. An observer asked, "Tell me, George, how many fish have you caught?"

"Well," the old fellow replied, "if I catch me this heah one I'm tryin' fo' and two more, I'll have three."

*   *   *   *

His mouth ain't no prayer book: Describes a fisherman's mouth...after the big one got away!

*   *   *   *

Herring: A fish with a name somewhat more acceptable than the crappie or the smelt. But that's not saying much. One thing is sure...they seem to look best with sour cream or when pickled.

*   *   *   *

And that almost-forgotten humorist, Eugene Field, wrote another nice one:

> I never lost a little fish —
> Yes, I am free to say.
> It always was the biggest fish
> I caught, that got away.

*   *   *   *

Fish should swim thrice: First, it should swim in the sea, then it should swim in butter, and, at last, it should swim in good claret.

— Jonathan Swift.

*   *   *   *

The biology teacher was explaining to his freshman high school class the spawning habits of fish: "And so it happens that the female fish deposits her eggs after which the male fish comes along and fertilizes them. Later, after a time, the fish hatch out."

One of the girls held up her hand. "Are you telling us, teacher, that the father and mother fish don't...that they don't...just don't do anything like...like, well, you know...before he fertilizes the eggs?"

"Nothing," replied the teacher.

One of the boys whispered to his buddy, "I bet that's how the phrase, 'a poor fish' got started."

* * * *

A banker and two of his customers went fishing in a small rowboat. A heavy squall came upon them and swamped the boat. Two of the men could swim, but the banker couldn't. He was sinking.

"Say, George," one of the customers called after seeing the banker floundering, "are you all right? Can you float alone?"

"You jerk!" screamed the banker, "here I am drowning and you want to talk business!"

* * * *

"George, did you fish with flies last weekend?"

"Did we fish with them! Sure did. We not only fished with them, we camped with them, ate with them, scratched with them and slept with them."

* * * *

A gracious plenty: Enough. In the above case...more than a *gracious plenty*.

* * * *

It was in the third grade that the teacher was explaining the fact that big fish eat little fish and little fish eat littler fish, and so on. "Are you saying that the bigger fish will eat even the small sardine, too?" asked one of the pupils.

"Yes," replied the teacher.

"Then tell me this, how in the world do they get the cans open?"

* * * *

The following is a story best not told to your lawyer. But, while fishing, a man fell overboard in shark-infested waters. He yelled for help, and a famous lawyer dove in to save him. In the process of towing the man to shore, sharks formed a two-lane convoy and escorted the lawyer, and the man he was towing, to shore.

Once ashore, the rescued man turned to the lawyer, exclaiming, "It's a miracle, a heaven-sent miracle!"

"Not at all," poo-pooed the lawyer. "It's just normal professional courtesy."

✳ ✳ ✳ ✳

"I wonder how Noah spent his time in the ark," a little boy asked in Sunday School class.

"Would anyone in the class like to hazard a guess about Noah and how he spent time on the ark?" the pastor asked.

"Probably he spent it fishing," said one classmate.

"Well, if he did he sure wouldn't catch many," volunteered yet another child.

"Why do you say that?" the minister asked.

"Well, you see, Noah only had two worms!"

✳ ✳ ✳ ✳

Angler: A guy who, first of all, lies in wait for a fish, then lies in weight after he lands it.

✳ ✳ ✳ ✳

Two professional fishermen got into an argument as to which one of them was best at mathematics. So they asked the captain of the fishing smack to decide. The captain suggested a problem to them, and whichever one got the answer first, that one would be the better mathematician.

"Figure that a crew caught 600 pounds of salmon and sold it at ninety cents a pound. How much would they take in?"

Well, the two fisherman got to work and figured with paper and pencil for more than an hour. Neither could come up with a solution. So they asked the captain to repeat the problem "If a fisherman caught 600 pounds of salmon...

"Wait a minute, Captain," interrupted one fisherman. "Do I understand that you said 'salmon'?"

"That's right."

"Hells bells, no wonder I couldn't figure it. I been figuring on mackerel all this time!"

* * * *

A poet was strolling alongside a river. He noticed a black man and boy fishing. But a moment later he saw the lad fall into the river and flounder about, obviously unable to swim. The black man jumped in and hauled him safely ashore where he began to pump the water out of the boy.

"That was noble of you," the poet congratulated the man. "Just superbly brave to risk your life to save that boy. It was sheer, heroic magnanimity!"

The black man smiled up at the poet and said, "Boss, I don't know eggzac'ly 'bout magnamaty, but if'n it mean dat dis boy heah had all de bait in his pocket, you' is sho nuff right."

* * * *

It is quite true that some men, when they tell a fish story, will go to any length.

* * * *

A fisherman had been fishing from the edge of a farm pond for about an hour when he became aware that a young lad was watching him from the bank above. The youngster finally asked, "How many fish have you caught, mister?"

"Haven't caught any, yet," the fisherman replied.

"Well," the boy said, "you ain't doin' bad at all. I seen a feller here who fished for two weeks in that same spot, and he didn't catch any more fish than you did in only one hour."

In a recent rural weekly newspaper, the following notice appeared: "Anyone found fishing in my pond at night will be found the next morning!"

✳ ✳ ✳ ✳

Fisherman: A gent who, by exaggeration, makes it a lot easier to swallow a fishbone than his fish story.

✳ ✳ ✳ ✳

The corner pharmacist was finding it hard to keep help. His sales volume did not justify paying standard wages, so he found it necessary to employ high school boys. He had long given up hope of training a teenager to be a good salesman. This time, when he hired a 16-year-old boy he said, "Sonny, there's one thing I want you to remember about selling. It's called the "related sale" and if you try to catch on to it, that's all I ask."

The boy did his best to learn. When the first customer came in and asked for some razor blades, the druggist put a package on the counter and said, "How are you fixed for shaving cream? And, by the way, we've got a special on after shave lotion today." The boy saw him build up a $5.00 sale to $10.00.

After a few days, the boy caught on to the "related sale" technique and was ready to tackle the next customer. This time it was a man who asked rather shyly for a box of sanitary napkins, naming one of the popular brands. The boy immediately went to work.

Just at that moment the telephone rang. When the pharmacist answered it, it proved to be a doctor with some rather complicated instructions about a number of complex prescriptions. This took considerable time. When the druggist finally returned to the front of the store, he was just in time to see the customer on his way out and up to his neck in packages. The young salesman was ringing up $500.95 on the cash register.

"What's this?" asked the amazed pharmacist.

"It's just a related sale, sir," answered the boy.

"Yes, yes, I know," said the pharmacist impatiently. "What in the world did you sell that man?"

"Well, I sold him the $250.00 fishing rod. And the $100 reel. And the pair of hip-waders. And a creel —"

"But good lord! All that man asked for was a box of sanitary napkins!"

"I know, I know, but as you told me to do, I gave him that old 'related sale' spiel," said the boy.

"Related sale?" yelled the dumbfounded pharmacist. "What did you say to him?"

"I just said," explained the boy, proudly, "look, mister, you're not going to be busy for the next few days. Why don't you go on a fishing trip?"

* * * *

A fisherman is a guy who catches a big fish by patience, and sometimes by luck, but most often by the...tale.

* * * *

The town banker had been fishing but had not caught a thing. On his way home, he stopped in the general store, went to the meat counter and asked the counterman to throw him six walleyes.

"What? You want me to throw you six walleyes? Can't I just wrap 'em and hand 'em to you?"

"No sir! Do as I tell you. When I get home I don't want anyone calling me a liar when I tell the family I caught six fish!'"

* * * *

"Holy smokes, I forgot the bait!" exclaimed the first fisherman.

"Are you kiddin'?" his buddy shot back. "How in the hell could you forget the most important...."

"Hells bells, man," the first fisherman interrupted, "you should have checked on it yourself. Because when I loaded the worms in the car...."

"Oh, you loaded the worms? I thought you were talking about the whiskey."

Fisherman: One who fishes till he's taken his fifth...then corks the bottle!

* * * *

A sign recently seen in the rear window of a fisherman's car.

"Warning...Fishing Pox. Very contagious to adult males.

"Symptoms: The patient complains constantly of a need for fresh air, for relaxation amidst sunshine and soft breezes. He has an oddly blank expression on his face and feels that he cannot do any work. He is forever checking the contents of his tackle box. He often hangs out in sporting goods stores far longer than he ever did before. And he mumbles to himself. Worse, he tells lies to everyone. There is no known cure except the following: "Victim must go fishing as soon and as often as possible."

* * * *

A fisherman was sitting on the bank of the Brule River, pulling on his hip boots and getting ready for some fun. The game warden drove up to him, stopped his pick-up truck, got out and asked to see the man's license. "I ain't fishin," the man replied. Then he stood, took his rod and reel and walked to the edge of the stream.

"Now let me see your dadblamed license!" the warden demanded.

"I still ain't fishin," the man said. Slowly he waded out into the stream until the water was almost to the top of his boots. Then he yelled to the warden, "Now I'm fishin', so if you still want to check on my license, come on out here, and do your checkin'!"

The preacher, a most enthusiastic fisherman, had been detained from his weekly fishing trip by a young couple insisting that he marry them immediately. He agreed, but not happily! Finally, the ceremony was almost over and the minister said, "Do you promise to love, honor and cherish this young lady, your intended?"

"I do," responded the bridegroom enthusiastically.

"Good," boomed the parson, turning toward the door, "then reel her in!"

* * * *

An American GI, on duty near the Arabian Sea, was fishing and hooked onto a dead weight. He reeled in and found that his hook had latched onto a cork in a bottle. When he had the bottle in the boat, he opened it and a huge genie popped out amidst a great cloud of purple smoke. "Ar- r-rgh!" yelled the genie, a monstrous figure, "I will take revenge for my imprisonment in that bottle on everybody I see. I'll kill them all. And you're the first!"

The quick-thinking GI said, "Go ahead. Kill me, you bastard. I won't believe — and neither will anyone else — that a silly jerk like you could be contained in such a tiny bottle. It is to laugh!"

"Oh yeah!" sneered the huge genie. "Guys like you, always doubting the obvious, burn me up! So you want proof, eh? Well, I'll show you I came out of there by getting back in." The genie shrunk himself to just the right size and jumped back in the bottle. The GI popped the cork back on it and threw the bottle back into the sea.

* * * *

Here's a poetic way to describe a man who is wasting his time: "He's fishin' with a rotten line and an empty hook!"

A man had ordered fish in a classy restaurant. But he sat and sat and the waiter did not bring his order. At last, after half an hour, the waiter appeared carrying a large silver platter, and with a flourish said, "This platter is for the next table. But your fish will be coming along in a minute or two, sir."

"Tell me," the irate customer asked, "just what kind of bait are you using?"

* * * *

A faht in a gale of wind, as in: "Them plastic flyrods is useless...ain't wuth *a faht in a gale of wind.*" (New England)

* * * *

What did the wife say to the returning fisherman? "Gesundheit! What else did you catch?"

* * * *

Two business partners took a day off and went fishing. Just as the fishing got good, one partner exclaimed, "Holy smokes, Ed! I forgot to lock the cash box."

"So what," his partner replied. "We're both here...so what's to worry?"

* * * *

The customer had ordered fish in the restaurant without knowing what kind of fish he would get. When it was served to him, he took a couple of bites and found it really tough and leathery.

"What kind of fish is this, anyway?" he asked the waiter.

"Filet of sole, sir," replied the walter.

"Do me a favor, waiter. Take this portion back to the kitchen and see if you can't get me a nice, tender piece of the upper, with the metal eyelets removed, of course."

Had the pork: In tough trouble, as, "When I couldn't fish out my huntin' license, I knew I'd *had the pork.*"

* * * *

Most fishermen don't stop to consider what an enormous debt they owe newspapers. To keep your pants clean, you sit on them. They make great fans to keep you cool. You wrap your fish in them to give to the neighbors. They make great fly and mosquito swatters. And for asswipe they can't be beat. How would we light campfires without them? There's no question about it...the hometown newspaper is the fisherman's best friend.

* * * *

What is an octopus? It is a fish built like a corporation.

* * * *

Fly: A single critter, one of millions manufactured to deceive, fool and obfuscate a desired fish. Present statistics illustrate that stupid fish have resolutely refused to bite on something like $4,036,594.26 worth of said flies during a single fishing session.

* * * *

There are still a lot of unbelievers when it comes to flying saucers. But Bill Montague swears that they exist because, one time he saw not one, but several. It seems that he came up behind a waitress who was carrying a full tray of dirty plates, and Bill had an extended fishing pole in his hand.

The following are two true, actual applications to the patent office. They are two examples of the many-sided, imaginative (and profit-conscious) American fisherman:

United States Patent Office

ARTIFICIAL FISH-BAIT

1,180,753 Specification of Letters Patent   Patented April 25, 1916
Application filed April 23, 1915. Serial No. 23,351

FIG. 1

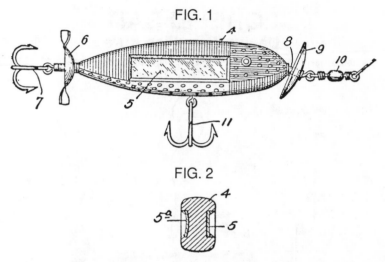

FIG. 2

...My invention relates more particularly to artificial baits for trawling, and its primary objects are to make the bait more attractive to the fish, to secure its proper position in the water, to provide a convenient and effective hanging of the hood, and to generally improve the structure and operation of trawling baits...

The attractiveness of the bait for the fish is increased by making the disks 6 and 9 of highly polished metal. The glitter and flashing lights occasioned by these and by the mirror are well known attractives; but the mirrors 5a and 5, is an additional feature that insures the effectiveness of the bait in the following manner: A male fish seeing his image upon looking therein will appear to see another fish approach it from the opposite side with the intent to seize the bait, and this will not only arouse his warlike spirit, but also appeal to his greed, and he will seize the bait quickly in order to defeat the approaching rival. In case the fish is suspected of cowardice, I may make the mirror of convex form, as shown in 5a, in order that the rival or antagonist may appear to be smaller. In the case of a female fish, the attractiveness of a mirror is too well known to need discussion. Thus the bait appeals to the ruling passion of both sexes, and renders it very certain and efficient in operation.

United States Patent Office

LORELEI BAIT
Design for a Fish Lure

Patented March 20, 1928 Dec. 74,759 Application filed November 19, 1927. Serial No. 24,209. Term of patent 7 years

| Figure 1 is a side elevation of a fish lure, showing my new design. | Figure 2 is a front elevation thereof. | Figure 3 is a longitudinal sectional view thereof... |

...Be it known that I...have invented a new, original, and ornamental Design for a Fish Lure, of which the following is a specification, reference being had to the accompanying drawing, forming part thereof.

ABSOLUTELY MAD INVENTIONS. A. E. Brown & H.A. Jeffcott, Jr. Dover Publications, New York. 1932.

HOW FISH GROW

Several months ago I had the unique experience of bass fishing with Jerry Meyer. While he was unsnarling a backlash, a bass swallowed his plastic worm.

When the fish made her first jump for freedom, it was obvious Jerry had a good one. He screamed for me to net the bass and I finally did.

I took the scales from my tackle box and weighed the flopping bass. I was happy for Jerry when I turned to him and said, "She weighs seven pounds even!"

Jerry instantly replied, "The bass weighs eight pounds!"

"No," I answered, "I checked the scales just last week. You have a seven-pound bass."

Jerry patiently explained that I had not allowed anything for shrinkage. A fish rapidly loses moisture when hauled from the water and this becomes a significant factor in determining true weight.

I told Jerry his bass had not been out of the water more than thirty seconds before I weighed her. She couldn't have dried out a pound that fast if she'd been in a washing-machine dryer.

Jerry said that I did not understand the chemistry of moisture loss. The bass had jumped three times before I netted her. On each jump, the fish was in the air long enough to have suffered dehydration, not to mention the net time. In addition, the bass had put on a three-minute battle under the water. The bass had expended considerable sudden energy and this caused drastic weight loss, plus the trauma of being hooked was bound to have resulted in bowel evacuation.

The bass was long and skinny. Jerry said she had not eaten in three days and that if she had only just fed on a school of minnows her true weight would be nine pounds. He said he was being conservative when he said the fish weighed eight pounds.

On the drive back from Lake Seminole to Albany, where I had left my car, Jerry stopped at twenty-two filling stations and bought a half-gallon of gas from each one. The attendants at each station noticed our fishing tackle.

They'd say, "You boys been fishing?"

Jerry would reply, "Yup."

"Catch anything?"

That's when Jerry would jump out, open the back of the station wagon, and take the lid off the ice chest. "I caught the big one!"

"What's it weigh?"

"A little under ten pounds."

I've often wondered how much that fish grew on Jerry's long drive to his home in Talking Rock, North Georgia. For all I know, by now it may have beaten George Perry's world record bass caught in 1932.

Fish biologists say that a largemouth bass does pretty well to grow one pound a year in a lake of average fertility. Under unusual conditions, a bass may gain two pounds or so in a year.

I think the biologists need to consult with Jerry Meyer. He showed me how a bass could grow a pound a minute.

Bass don't stop growing after they are dead. In fact, that may be their period of most rapid growth.

I've learned a lot from Jerry and other technical experts. They don't measure by the metric or the American system. They have their own: Two fish equal a stringer, five fish equal a big stringer, and seven ounces equal a pound.

For a number of years it was a constant source of embarrassment to me that as an outdoor writer, I had never caught a trophy bass, one weighing ten pounds or more. I had seen several anglers who had achieved this, and actually touched one of them, but it had never happened to me. In the tradition of all true Southerners, I went out one night and changed my luck. The next day I caught a largemouth which weighed 11 1/4 pounds.

I am sure she weighed this much because I tested her on four sets of scales. On the first three, she weighed 11 even, but I did not mind driving the twenty miles until I found a set where she pulled 11 1/4 pounds.

I did not allow anything for shrinkage, one reason being that the two buddies with me did not believe the theory. They did admit the bass was long and lanky and if she had been fat and full of eggs she would have weighed considerably more.

Since my wife had always wanted a stuffed bass for our living room, I had the fish mounted. When it came back from the taxidermist, the long, skinny fish had turned into a stocky one with a sagging belly, obviously one which weighed twelve or thirteen pounds in the raw.

Unfortunately, at my request, the taxidermist had installed a bronze nameplate stating where the fish had been caught, the date, and weight. I hung the fish in a dark part of the living room where an admirer could not get in reading range of the plate without leaning across a table studded with broken bottles.

Whenever an unexpected visitor, such as the paperboy, came to our home, I would take him into the living room and modestly point at the bass. No matter who the visitor, even the garbage collector, he would always ask how much the fish weighed.

I was always totally honest and would reply, "A little under twelve pounds."

The trouble was that some of the admirers would notice the plate and edge around and read the 11 1/4 pounds. I decided to remove the plate. The trouble was that it left a mark, as though the mount had been tampered with.

When I had the bass transferred to a new wooden mount, with no plate giving away the weight, my bass both gained and lost weight, depending on my visitor. The trick was to get the visitor to say what the largest bass he ever caught weighed before he asked me how much my mounted one weighed.

If the largest bass weighed ten pounds, mine weighed 10 1/4. If another said his record bass was twelve pounds, mine was 12 1/4. The most my bass has ever weighed is 15 1/2 pounds. I never beat their records by more than one-quarter of a pound. It's one thing to be flexible, but I don't believe in lying!

Opening Shots And Parting Lines. Charley Dickey Winchester Press. 1983

✳ ✳ ✳ ✳

Bing Crosby returned from a fishing trip to Colorado, and he was asked how things had gone with the fish in those parts.

Bing remained silent a few moments, then replied, "I can't really tell you that. You see, for two weeks I dropped them a line twice a day...but I got not one reply."

Straight ahead: OK! You bet! Sure enough! As, "You want to go fishin' Sunday? *Straight ahead.* Pick me up at 5 AM."

* * * *

Anyone who has owned a cranky, troublesome motorboat will understand this fisherman's description of his fishing boat that was always in the shop for repairs. He summed up the matter cryptically: "A boat is a hole in the water into which you constantly throw money!"

* * * *

Going to a hunting and fishing convention with your wife is like going fishing with the game warden.

* * * *

Two fishermen had returned from a day's fishing with the allowed limit of bass. The optimist was ecstatic about their fun. "It couldn't have been better," he explained. "What a great day."

But the other fisherman, the pessimist, added: "I figure it coulda been better...if...well, it coulda rained tartar sauce!"

* * * *

Talk about tough luck. There's this fellow in upper Wisconsin who caught a giant muskie. The poor guy dislocated both shoulders describing it.

* * * *

Projeckin: Cuttin'-up, as "He wasn't much at fishin' but good at *projeckin'* round the fire come nighttime." (a cowboy's phrase.)

* * * *

With the bark on: To tell it exactly as it was. A difficult task for fishermen.

Sizzle-Sozzler: A heavy rain but no goose-drownder, as, "Sure wish we'd get us a real *sizzle-sozzler* to relieve this-eyer drought!"

* * * *

Wife: "Well, my dear, did you catch a lot of fish on your trip up north?"

Hubby: (Who had spent three days on a glorious drunk and hadn't wet a line) "Had a great time, dear. And did we catch fish! Wow! But we gave 'em all to Goodwill. They always need help, y' know. But that reminds me...you forgot to pack my shaving stuff and my toothbrush."

Wife: "They were all," she replied acidly, "in your tackle box!"

* * * *

Wise men say that the sport of fishing is simplicity itself. All you must do is get there yesterday when the fish were biting. But who is to know? One fellow who picked the wrong day was seen to throw away his pole and begin to hop around on one foot, howling in great pain. The father of a seven-year-old boy discovered this fellow in all anguish.

"What happened?" the father of the boy asked. "It's all my fault, Dad," the kid said. "You see this man told me he hadn't had a bite all morning...so I bit him."

* * * *

A kind-hearted fellow was walking through Central Park in New York and was astonished to see an old man, fishing rod in hand, fishing over a beautiful bed of lilies. 'Tch" 'Tch!" said the passerby to himself. "What a sad sight. That poor old man is fishing over a bed of flowers. I'll see if I can help." So the kind fellow walked up to the old man and asked, "What are you doing, my friend?"

"Fishin',sir."

"Fishing, eh. Well, how would you like to come have a drink with me?"

The old man stood, put his rod away and followed the kind stranger to the corner bar. He ordered a large glass of beer and a fine cigar. His host, the kind fellow, felt good about helping the old man, and he asked, "Tell me, my old friend, how many did you catch this morning?"

The old fellow took a long drag on the cigar, blew a careful smoke ring and replied, "You are the sixth, sir."

* * * *

Fixin': Just about to do it, as, "Didn't have to work today so I was *fixin'* to tie flies."

* * * *

There is an ardent fisherman in Manhattan who is also a competent obstetrician. This physician, on his way home from a fishing trip, received an emergency call and rushed to the hospital. He delivered the baby in good shape, and the anxious father was impatient to know how much the baby weighed. The only scale the doctor had was the one he used to weigh fish. Can you imagine the surprise of the father when he discovered the doctor had weighed in his baby at 32 pounds!

* * * *

The fisherman pulled up to a small bait shop and asked the owner, "Are there any big fish being caught in Lake Tomahawk?"

"Are there? Wow, you bet! Why lately, they've had to hide boys and small men behind trees before they let 'em bait a hook. Yep! Them fish'll attack 'em to get the worms."

* * * *

Milkin' time: Time for a drink (5 PM), as, "It's *milkin' time,* fellers. Let's quit fishin' and git to it."

"SO I HAVE A LITTLE ACCURACY PROBLEM WITH MY CASTING..."

He looks like a suck-up dawg: What a fisherman's face look like when he gets a walleye up to the boat and then loses it. You could say, also, "he's mad as a settin' hen."

*   *   *   *

For many years, fishermen had tried to take a giant catfish they named "The Monster." They got together and devised a can't-miss bait and, after days of effort, actually landed this big daddy. It may have been that age was acting in their favor because the whiskers of this catfish were pure white. He was some old!

Well, the entire community rejoiced. They had a big feast and then salted down the remains that kept the entire village in food for two and a half years.

Not only did they feed off that fish for years, but they used his scales for shingles. His ribs formed the floor joists for 15 new homes, and the remaining shingles were used to start a new industry...The Shovel Company. You see, the back bone was split into many sections that formed the handles of shovels. And, the excess shingles formed the scoops! Now, you got to admit that The Monster was one heckovafish.

* * * *

I'd like to buy him for what he's worth and sell him for what he thinks he's worth: A way to describe a conceited ass who'll never again be invited to go fishing with the boys!

* * * *

THE YOUNGSTER'S QUERY

An answer to this question
Is what I greatly wish;
Does fishing make men liars —
Or do only liars fish?

* * * *

No frustrated and luckless fisherman could ask for a nicer obituary on his tombstone than this true one:

He angled many a purling brook,
But lacked an angler's skill:
He lied about the fish he took,
And here he's lying still.

* * * *

Gritchel: What you keep your gear in when you go for a week's fishin'. A combination of grip and satchel.

* * * *

Fisherman's motto: Don't hurry...settle back...then bait and see.

Ed Zern gave this apt description of the tall tale genre in "To Hell With Hunting," back in 1946:

"A number of theories have been advanced to account for that time-honored American institution, the tall story. Some of the professors claim that the early inhabitants were overwhelmed by the vastness of the country and tried to tell all their stories to match. Other authorities on folk humor (most of whom haven't cracked a smile since the day the dog et grandmaw) declare that Americans tell tall stories to relieve a national inferiority complex.

"My own theory is simpler and consists of two demonstrable premises: 1 - that practically all Americans are natural-born liars. And 2 - that it is more fun to lie big than to lie little."

**   *   *   ***

Here are two tales from Professor Roger Welsch's superb book of Nebraska tall tales: *SHINGLING THE FOG.* Roger Welsch. University of Nebraska Press. Lincoln,NE and London. 1972.

Alfred H. Ulrich of Wayne County, Nebraska, was caught in one of those typical Plains storms we often hear about that followed him home from town so close "that, although not one drop of water fell on him as he sat in the buggy, the hind wheels were running in six inches of water...!

"When he got home he found a fish in the back end of his buggy. He put it in a jar to keep it for a pet but soon got tired of changing the water for it every day and he decided that it could live without water. He poured out a little of the water every day until the fish finally was used to living on dry land. Then he kept it in the canary cage and after a few meals of canary seed it could whistle like a bird and seemed to be perfectly happy.

"One day, however, when the radio set was tuned in, an orchestra was playing the *Star Spangled Banner,* the poor fish tried to stand up and fell into the drinking water, and before Mr. Ulrich would reach it, it had drowned. The poor fish!"

In addition to the sorrow which all readers must also feel, I cannot help but wonder if the fish in the Nebraska story, eating canary seed was ever induced to lay eggs in a nest.

As the wild fish acquired their share of wiliness, they applied their knowledge in the never-ending struggle against crafty Plains fishermen: "A man was fishing when a huge fish got on his line. It was so big in fact that he called for help. A skindiver not far away heard his call and went to see if he might be of help. The fisherman suggested he dive down and see how large the fish was. He went down and soon came back with the report that it was a very large fish, but that it swam inside an old car body and so lodged there. Picking up a stick, the fisherman asked if he would please dive down and poke him out with the stick. The skindiver took the stick and disappeared into the water. When he returned to the fisherman he reported that he had no luck, for everytime he tried to give the fish a poke with the stick, he'd roll up the windows on the car."

As was also the case with the rattlesnakes, pioneers found that fish given half a chance, could prove to be compassionate, sensitive, and grateful fellow-creatures:

W. Harrison Stephens of Nuckolls County tells of a fishing trip which he took on the Cedar River two years ago.

"I caught a four-foot bass, but upon seeing the appealing look in the fish's eyes I promptly threw it back into the water. When I reached home, I discovered the loss of a valuable watch.

"Two years passed by and I returned to the same river. While idly casting my line into the water I noticed a large bass circling about the boat. Suspecting something, I waited, and to my surprise the fish brought my lost watch to the surface. The watch was running! Marks on the stem indicated that the faithful bass had daily wound the watch and it was only five minutes slow."

I once had much the same experience while fishing on the Loup River near Fullerton, Nebraska. I, too, lost a fine German watch and fully expected that it was gone forever. About two years later, while boating on that river with some colleagues, I caught (to their envy) a fine 22-inch catfish, with much the same look on his face as the one I had set free the fishing trip two years earlier. Imagine my surprise when opening him the next morning for breakfast to find a complete set of entrails.

"How do you want it—broiled or mounted?"

Upstream, Downstream and Out of My Mind. Syd Hoff. © 1961

Back in 1945, John Randolph wrote a book of TEXAS BRAGS and it was a doozy. Here is his "Fishy" brag from the book.

FISHY
Over 230 Kinds

Texas has over 120 varieties of fresh water fish and over 110 salt water species.

Over 3900 rivers, bayous and lakes to fish in — to say nothing of the Gulf of Mexico.

Is it any wonder that the biggest and truest fish stories come from Texas?

There are towns named Fish, Pike, Sturgeon, Crane, Eagle, Goldfinch, Lark, Peacock, Quail, Swan and Turkey

The Rio Grande, which forms the southern border of Texas, winds 1,569 miles to the Gulf of Mexico.

Texas has 973 miles of coast on the Gulf.

Texas has the world's largest smallest river. The Comal River rises in the city of New Braunfels and before it leaves town it empties into the Guadalupe River — empties 220,000,000 gallons of water daily.

"Any luck?"

Upstream, Downstream and Out of My Mind. Syd Hoff. © 1961

F.D.R. was an ardent fisherman and fishing in the River Brule was one of his favorite ways of relaxing from his presidential duties.

Returning from one of these excursions to Washington, the President was asked if he had had any luck.

"Well," replied the President, "I estimate that there are forty-five thousand fish in the Brule River, and although I haven't caught them all yet, I've intimidated them."

* * * *

President Coolidge was officiating at the laying of a cornerstone. He turned a shovelful or two of dirt with the golden ceremonial shovel while the crowd watched with reverential silence. The President paused, peered down in the hole.

"That's a fine fishworm," he remarked, smiling.

President Cleveland was an ardent fisherman, and it is said that he enjoyed angling for the fish that would not bite quite as much as he did for those that would. While fishing one day, dressed in oilskins and a slouch hat, he was addressed by an angler garbed in the height of piscatorial fashion with:

"Hello, boatman! You've certainly got a good catch. What will you take for the fish?"

"I'm not selling them," replied the man in oilskins.

"Well," continued the persistent angler, "do you want to take me out fishing tomorrow?"

Mr. Cleveland, who was plainly enjoying the joke, replied, "I can't make any engagements except by the season. Will you give me as much as I made last year?"

"You're a sharp fellow," replied the angler, "But a good fisherman, and I'll accept your terms. What did you make last year?"

"Oh," replied Mr. Cleveland, "about a thousand dollars a week! I was the President of the United States."

✳   ✳   ✳   ✳

We are all familiar with the Ten Commandments. There's a new one proposed by a fisherman fined fifty dollars for fishing on posted grounds. It reads, "Thou Shalt Not Fish Here."

✳   ✳   ✳   ✳

Fishing: Eternal   optimism   and   never-ending disappointment.

✳   ✳   ✳   ✳

A veteran fishing guide in Minnesota was asked if he'd ever been lost in the dense woods of the Superior National Forest.

"Nope," he replied, "I ain't never been whatcha call lost. But they was a couple of days once when I was mighty confused!"

A rich lady, given to what were once called "hoity toity society doin's," once read that fish were a marvelous food to improve the function of the brain. So she went to her doctor to verify the fact and to get advice on the kind, amount, frequency of eating this wonderful brain food.

"I'd dearly love to improve my mind, Doctor," she said, "but I need your advice on the details of consuming fish to improve my mind."

"Not complicated in your case," the physician said. "Just take a baby whale on toast every morning!"

* * * *

There was a young fellow named Fisher,
Who was fishing for fish in a fissure,
When a cod with a grin
Pulled the fisherman in,
Now they're fishing the fissure for Fisher.

* * * *

Scrid: A wee bit more, as, "I'll take just a *scrid* of trout, cookie."

* * * *

It has been observed that if fishermen talked only about the fish they really caught, the silence would be unbearable.

* * * *

Definition of a mermaid: An oh boy! girl upstairs and a fish downstairs. Still others have defined her as a "Wet dream!"

* * * *

Back in 1965, Charles Andres III, told Argosy of an unusual experience he had while fishing in the boonies. He wrote, "What do you do with a record fish on your hands when you have no refrigeration and the plane picks you up six days later?"

"This was my situation last September. Finally, in desperation, I succumbed to Al's assurance that my fish would keep if I gave it a thick coat of our cooking grease (we had Crisco), wrapped it thoroughly to make it airtight and buried it in a shady place.

"Of course, the first thing I did when we returned to civilization was to register my prize. Much to my consternation and disbelief, my fish measured in as a close second! It was three inches shorter than when I first measured it. There were no errors in the first measurement or in the calibration of my tape.

"I did write to and got an answer from the Crisco people. They said, 'The next time, don't use shortening.'"

* * * *

Toost: To lift, as "I held the rod real good and *toosted* that fish right into the boat."

* * * *

There was once a fisherman who was gone from home so much that his wife moved for a divorce. He told her he'd do anything for her if she'd only stay with him. What did she want? She asked for a Jaguar. He hurried out and bought one for her. He presented his gift to her and derned if the critter didn't eat her up!

* * * *

While stationed in the Pacific during World War II, an old native islander, John B. Thomas, showed a way to catch fish without any equipment but his bare hands. It had been a jealously guarded secret, but now that his future is assured, he has revealed it to the Honest Abe Club.

You place your hand in a stream, palm up, and wait until a fish swims across it. Then, by gently manipulating your fingers, you proceed to tickle the belly of the fish until the fish becomes helpless with hysterical laughter. Now, all that is left is for you to scoop it up out of the water into whatever kind of receptacle you have handy.

I myself do not eat fish, so I do this only as a hobby.

One fish I caught in this manner laughed so loud that I decided to keep him for a pet. He (or she, whatever it is) has provided me with a source of income for many years to come. I made a tape recording of it laughing and have since sold this tape to television. Anyone who may doubt my word can turn on their TV set to any of the comedy shows and listen to the canned laughter. When they become suspicious and the laughter sounds fishy that's the tape of my pet.

✱ ✱ ✱ ✱

A fisherman once asked his minister if it was a sin to fish on Sunday. The minister replied: "From the information I have concerning the few fish you catch, it's a sin any day you go fishing."

✱ ✱ ✱ ✱

Fishy tall tales? Yes. Funny fish stories? Of course. Rowdy fish cartoons? Often. But fish puns? Hardly. Yet, just look at this odd combination from Bennett Cerf's great collection: *A TREASURY OF ATROCIOUS PUNS.*

FISH STORY

The prettiest she-fish in the whole aquarium was Bess Porgy. Young John Haddock's gills fluttered with suppressed poison every time she and her chubby friend Mazie Angelfish slithered down the pike. To kipper in comfort was his consuming obsession.

Trouble loomed, however, when the two girls worked out a sister act and opened at the Globe under the management of Salmon & Schuster. An interested member of the audience was Rufus Goldfish, who sat in the second roe (he was slightly hard of herring) and viewed the performance with a sardinic smile. "Confidentially," he told a grouper friends later, "the girls act smelt, but they're pretty cute tricks. I found the one who was barracuda."

John Haddock's sole shriveled at these words. "Only an act of cod will keep my Bess out of his clutches," he muttered shadly. Miss Angelfish tried to rally him. "Don't be blue," she counseled. "You are no common weakfish. You are a Haddock. Remember Dorothy Vernon of Haddock Hall. Get in there and put that bass sailfish, old flounder, t'rout!"

John squared what passes for shoulders in a fish. "Thanks, Mazie," he spluttered. "By gum and bivalve, I'll get out of this pickerel yet. If that shrimp expects to mackerel have me to reckon with!"

Suiting the action to the words, he knocked his rival off his perch so effishently that poor Mr. Goldfish whaled for the carps — and a sturgeon to get the bones out of his mouth.

"I did it on porpoise," cried the exultant John Haddock, clasping Bess, who looked prettier than Marlin Dietrich, to his slippery chest.

It was all such a shark to Mr. Goldfish that he's been eel to this very day.

The Haddocks had a tarpon time of it ever after.

✳ ✳ ✳ ✳

Donald Saab developed a system for catching fish without the use of hook, line or sinker. Here's his inventive technique:

"You get yourself a clear glass gallon jug with a handle on it, fill it with clear water, put a minnow in it and close the top. Then tie a six- to eight-foot rope to the jug handle and head for your favorite fishing spot. Tie the other end of the rope to a branch of a tree — or on the side of your boat — and drop the jug in the water.

"The fish will dive for the minnow and bang their heads against the jug, so all you have to do is pick them up before they regain consciousness."

Fishin' stories haven't changed in 2500 years. The Greeks, too, used to listen to lyres.

✳ ✳ ✳ ✳

There was an avid ice fisherman from Vermont who devised one of the neatest systems for indulging his sport. Here's how he does it:

"I cut a hole in the ice — hold a watch over the hole, and when the fish come up to see what time it is I hit them over the head."

✳ ✳ ✳ ✳

It is simply amazing the techniques that intelligent, cerebral fishermen have adapted to enhance their sport. Just read about this ultrasonic technique in the hands of moral and conservation-minded Bill Anderson:

"This friend of mine, an electronics engineer, has a large fishing boat which he has equipped with all the latest marine navigational equipment, such as radar, radio telephone, direction finder and depth sounder. Only one of these devices, however, is pertinent to this story. It's the depth sounder. You can forget about the others. They don't work, anyway. Batteries are too weak. The reason the batteries are too weak is because my friend has the depth sounder going all the time, trying to locate fish with it.

✳ ✳ ✳ ✳

"As you know, a depth sounder sends out ultrasonic signals called 'pings' which go straight down in the water until they hit something solid, then an echo bounces back up to the boat, where it is recorded on an indicator showing the depth and type of the object. Since fish are solid objects, their bodies reflect the pings back to the surface and are duly registered by the indicator as genuine, lifelike, realistic fish-type fish.

"Unfortunately, as my friend discovered, these very pings which locate the fish also irritate them, causing them to lose whatever appetite they might otherwise have had. After all, Who enjoys being pinged at? Nobody. Not even fish. Maybe especially not fish.

"At least, that's what my friend got to brooding over and that's why he developed a modified depth sounder that would be more pleasing to the fish. The one he built doesn't go 'ping' anymore. By adding another circuit that goes 'ork' he was able to combine the two sounds so that, when the signal reaches the fish, it sounds more like 'pork' — which everyone knows is a very appetizing signal indeed to many different species of fish.

"A word of warning, however. As my friend points out, fishermen who use this system must be sure actually to have a chunk of pork on their lines or the fish will soon learn to distrust men as a whole and look upon all fishermen as a deceitful lot. And we can't have that sort of rumor going around!"

* * * *

For many years the fishermen of Lake Matoxie had tried to land a huge black bass, but always, this brute of a fish managed to get away taking, in most cases, hook, line and sinker with him. As was inevitable, that wily fish made a mistake and got caught. But Mr. Fish might as well have stayed free for all the good he did for the guy who caught him. You see, the bass was so derned full of fishhooks and lead weights that the fellow had to sell him for scrap iron!

* * * *

Lest the preceding story seem a bit strange, let us consider another true tale but almost the reverse of the foregoing.

* * * *

A fly-fisherman was trying a certain stream that was limited to just that...the use of flies...only flies! And this fellow caught what he thought was a record bass, long, broad and thick. So he took his prize fish to the weight station for record fish and that fish only weighed one-and-a-half pounds.

Shocked, the fisherman had expected at least a nine pound bass. He cleaned the fish and then understood the problem. That bass was packed full of flies he taken off fisherman over the course of many years. He was literally packed full of feathers and feathers don't weigh much. So, you see, all is not bass that bites.

* * * *

Jo-jeezley: Used in place of profanity, as, "I have never seen water so *jo-jeezley* rough as this lake is."

"FIVE YEARS!.....OR TELL ME WHERE YOU CAUGHT HIM!"

AN UNKNOWN POET'S EULOGY FOR THE WORM

The angleworm's the friend of man,
The mascot of the garden,
Yet anglers toss him in a can
And never beg his pardon.
I unreservedly affirm
They don't do right by that poor worm.

The angleworm's a harmless cuss
And keeps the humus fertile,
But when they see him, quite a fuss
Is made by Mae and Myrtle.
He lacks the caterpillar's fuzz —
But handsome is as handsome does.

Think kindly of the angleworm,
Be gentle when you meet him,
And give a sympathetic squirm
When greedy robins eat him.
Let this thought govern what you do —
He never done no dirt to you!

＊　＊　＊　＊

A terrific storm came over the Superior National Forest area and swamped the canoe in which were two fellows fishing. They managed to swim to shore but were many miles from their supplies. "How on earth did you survive?" the girlfriend asked.

"It sure wasn't easy," her boyfriend replied. "Luckily, my partner, Pete Joust, had a can of sardines in his pocket, and we lived on that for a week."

"Both of you lived on one can of sardines for a week?" the lady exclaimed.

"Yep!"

"How on earth did you both keep from falling off!"

＊　＊　＊　＊

Mud season: Between spring and summer, as, "The best fishin' is in *mud season.*"

＊　＊　＊　＊

School breakin': End of school term, as, "Now that *school breakin'* done come, you and them kids'll be fishin' every creek and pond in the county."

A fellow named George told the following story. It simply has to be true because anyone named George (remember St. George?) must be a teller of true tales and only...true...tales.

One day, while fishing my favorite part of a lake, I noticed a school of fish near what appeared to be a large log. I stopped the boat and threw my double-edged anchor over the side.

While tying my favorite lure on my line, I noticed that the anchor rope began to get taut. Soon the boat began to move. Looking into my fish monitor, I noticed the large log was now moving.

I quickly started my 80-horse motor and began to fight whatever was on the other end of the anchor's line. After running out eight gallons of gas, the fish finally tired, and I was able to pull him to the shore. It was the largest catfish I had ever seen.

I loaded the fish on a two-ton flat-bed truck and drove it back to my home town of 2,500 people. I decided to use an old abandoned brick warehouse, which belonged to a friend, to smoke my catch. I invited the whole town to a fish fry the following day.

A number of the town folk thanked me for the fine meal. A few of the envious fishermen of the community came to my table to console me about not being able to mount such a fine catch for use over the fireplace.

* * * *

I, of course, had the last laugh! I still had the 25 1/2 pound bass that swallowed my anchor and was bait for that catfish!

* * * *

Ugly enough to curdle milk: As, "Them catfish is *ugly enough to curdle milk*" or "ugly as a mud fence."

* * * *

The question is often asked as to the difference between a fishing rod and a fishing pole. Quite simple. A fishing rod costs more than $100.

There's a feller in Nelson, Wisconsin, who told this lolapaloozer. He was talkin' about the recent dry spell that had come over Wisconsin. "Why, fellers," this whopper-teller said, "the water in the lake where I do most of my fishin' got so blamed low that my boat quit leakin'."

* * * *

Fisherman: A native species who, unlike Africans who fish lying down, almost always lies standing up with a maximum outstretch of the arms.

* * * *

Sizzle-sozzler: A heavy rain but no goose-drownder, as, "Sure wish we'd get us a *sizzle-sozzler.* Makes for good fishin'."

* * * *

A big lineside bass that lived in Bull Creek not far from Rockaway Beach, was called "Jingle-Bells" because he carried so many hooks and spinners in his massive jaws that they actually jingled like sleighbells whenever he broke water. Nearly every fisherman at the beach had hooked the huge fish, but he always got away somehow. Finally, a tourist who watched with binoculars from a high tree solved the problem. A big crawpappy always rode on Jingle-Bells' back and whenever the fish was hooked the crawpappy cut the line with his sharp pincers! My old friend George Hall heard about it, and rung in a wire leader on him. The poor old crawpappy did his best, but finally had to give up and drop off, leaving Jingle-Bells to his fate. The great bass went to the kitchen at last, and his collection of hooks and lures is still on exhibition in Captain Bill's hotel at Rockaway.

* * * *

Split the quilt: Divorce, separate, as, "He goes fishin' lots more since he *split the quilt.*"

Baldy Huntoon caught the biggest rainbow trout ever taken at Roaring River — he told me so himself, in a bawdy-house at Joplin. It seems that Baldy, when he first sighted the fish, perceived that it was too long to turn around in the channel. So he straddled the stream at a narrow point and threw some stones into the water ahead of the fish. There was nothing for the monster to do but back slowly upstream and as it passed under Baldy, he mounted it just as one would a horse. Before the big fish could get away, Huntoon stuck his thumbs into its gill-slits and throwed it right out on the bank!

*   *   *   *

Tall-Tale Teller: A fisherman who tells the truth about the exact weight of a fish he almost caught.

*   *   *   *

Fishing: The one solitary vice that men may enjoy without shame.

*   *   *   *

A boatman on the lower White River sold me a mess of very large frog legs. I remarked upon their phenomenal size, but he replied that the really big frogs had been killed off years ago. "When I was a young-un," said he, "the croakers in these here bottoms were big as full-grown steers. We used to butcher 'em just like hogs, an' salt 'em down for winter. They was so God-awful big we had to slice up their legs like a quarter of beef an' cut through the bone with a bucksaw. When they got to bellerin' of a night, they'd rattle the winder-glass ten mile off! Them big 'uns could jump two hundred yards, easy. I've saw 'em jump one hundred yards, straight up in the air, to ketch a chicken-hawk!"

Now, if those foregoing Vance Randolph tales seem almost too tall, consider this story, warranted true by a Little Rock, Arkansas, justice of the peace back in 1904. Although a feller named Hughes related it back then, his devotion to facts seems unrelated to that of the Hughes, who was our former Chief Justice of the U.S. Supreme Court.

A CURIOUS MATTER

When it comes to catching large fish, Arkansas has all the states beat. The largest fish I ever saw, read, or heard tell of, was caught out of the Arkansas River below Little Rock. It kept getting their bait and breaking their lines. Finally they had a blacksmith to make a fish-hook out of a crowbar; they tied it to a steamboat cable and baited it with a muly cow that had died with the holler horn, tied the cable to a tree, and the next morning they had him; they was afraid he would pull a team in the river, so they got all the Negroes for miles around and pulled him out on the bank, and hauled him to town in sections. When they cut him open they found inside of him another fish that weighed two hundred pounds (by guess), three fat hogs, one yoke of oxen, and an acre of burnt woods.

— Marion Hughes (1904)

From kin see to kaint see: Dawn to dark, as "We fished *from kin see to kaint see*."

* * * *

Of the sources for tall tales, the Burlington, Wisconsin, Liar's Club excels them all. Still on active duty after more than 50 years of service to that part of the American community that loves the fine art of whoppers and windies, the Burlington Liar's Club will go on as Americans cherish the wit and humor that is typically theirs. And no form of that humor is more typically American than the tall tale. Here are six tales from members of the club.

— The Burlington Liars Club

* * * *

The birds were flying too high to shoot at, one huntin' day. Then a typical Wisconsin stream mosquito buzzed down into my duck blind, grabbed me by the collar and carried me straight up into the air where the mallards were flying. I shot my limit and the mosquito returned me to the blind. Then he flew around the swamp retrieving the ducks and before leaving for good, counted the ducks to make sure I got 'em all!

— The Burlington Liars Club

* * * *

After ten years of thrilling, but unsuccessful efforts to capture a particular fish, I decided to follow it in its course in the spring and summer of 1932. I followed it down the Tensaw River until it arrived at the Gulf Stream in Mobile.

After using machine guns, dynamite and, with the assistance of the lock-tender, 100 men and 200 boys, I finally captured and landed the fish. There were no scales in Alabama that could weigh it, and I have forgotten its exact dimensions, except that it measured 92 feet between the eyes. When we pulled it out, it took 48 hours for the hole in the water to fill up. I shall always regret deeply that I did not let that fish alone till it was full grown.

— John Bookhardt

Stemmy: Horny, sexy, libidinous, as, "It is true that oysters make you stemmy? Old Pete thought so. He et six of them for dinner on his weddin' night, but only five of them worked."

* * * *

I had a trained pike I used in the White River that was so canny I never took any bait to go fishing. Better than bait, the pike would lead other large pike to my especially painted hooks.

The water up above the mill dam is so clear you can always see what's going on below. One Fourth of July, I caught 27 pike weighing over three pounds. Each and every one of them came up with my own trained fish. He used to tease them along, make a dart for the fake bait and then nibble on a corner I left out for him. The other fellow would rush in and gobble it up to beat him to it, and then all I had to do was pull the line out.

* * * *

Slicker'n a smelt: Easily, as, "I horsed that walleye outa there *slicker'n a smelt*."

* * * *

The American talent for solutions to problems of how to catch fish is of genius quality and never-ending in its quest. Just consider this scientific fisherman who must remain anonymous because he does not want others coming to him to learn how to catch vast quantities of fish by using this method. He is a sincere conservationist and asks that the readers of this book keep the entire matter confidential.

This fellow understood that bass were terrific fighters, pugnacious beyond belief. The bass is like an Irishman and fights at the drop of an eyelid — or for no reason at all.

But this fisherman used his brain. He figured how to use the fighterliness of the bass to catch him. And so he uses mirrors. He lowers a mirror into the water, and the bass, seeing a reflection of another bass, attacks! He charges hard at that image in the mirror, bangs his head with such abandon that he knocks himself unconscious, and it is then easy to pick him up off the bottom of the creek. This clever fisherman explains his slightly stooped shoulders as due to the enormous loads of bass, caught by the mirror-method, that over the years he has had to carry home.

* * * *

The editor thought the above story kind of frightening until another one came over the wire. In this case, a horde of New Jersey mosquitoes descended on tents in which fishermen were spending the night. Well, sir, those blamed mosquitoes stripped off all the canvas and took the ropes with them into the night, leaving the fishermen totally uncovered.

In the morning the fishermen headed for the base camp to get some replacement tents. While enroute, paddling away, they saw an amazing sight. Those same mosquitoes were flying about, on shore, togged out in Canvas Slacks and Suspenders. The tent ropes? You guessed it. They'd made Bow Ties out of them! Now if that doesn't beat all...still one wonders why they avoided canvas sports shoes. Not dressy enough?

* * * *

And yet another story that, if misapplied, could seriously deplete our stock of fish. The mirror story was bad enough. But this one is frightening.

A high-binder had manufactured a sure-fire hair-restorer. It worked quite well on all his buddies who had become bald. So he loaded a fifty gallon barrel of the hair restorer on the bed of his pick-up truck. In crossing an old, rough bridge, the barrel upset and spilled into one of the finest trout streams in the country.

Not long after the hair-restorer spill, the folks in the vicinity noticed that the fish began to grow beards and that all they had to do was to put up a barber chair, set a striped pole in the ground, holler "Next!" and those stupid fish would come out for a shave. Yep! But think a minute. Suppose that this got to be a common procedure everywhere? Common as bait-casting, for example. Well! We'd soon be out of fish, wouldn't we? So join us in petitioning Congress to outlaw the use of hair-restorer in streams as a means to catch fish. We demand that every barber chair and every barber pole be licensed and possessed only by licensed barbers who are non-fishermen. If you wish to join our Ban The Barber Chair movement, please contact the editor!

✳ ✳ ✳ ✳

"How's fishin' in these parts?"

"T'was real good till the wind come up strong."

"Really? Just how strong was it?"

"Well, cookin' breakfast this morning, the wind blew so hard it took our well right out of the ground, sucked the stove up the stovepipe, pulled the kitchen out the window and then mixed the days of the week so bad that Sunday didn't come till Tuesday night. And you ask how's fishin'?"

✳ ✳ ✳ ✳

The great Audubon once labeled a fish that he saw, "The Devil Jack Diamond Fish." The fish frequented most American rivers where it grew to enormous size. But most remarkable were its marvelous scales, shaped like cut-diamonds that were set in oblique rows. And they were so tough a rifle bullet could not penetrate them. Once they were dry, you could strike fire by striking steel against them.

After James Audubon (1785-1851) released this information, a contemporary Englishman informed his readers of still other remarkable fish in America. His thoroughly scientific and verified findings are as follows:

There are a great number of fishes in the Mississippi, some of which are unsuited for food, but are curious in other respects. One of these is called the alligator-gar, or lepiosteus ferox; it is found sometimes exceeding eight feet in length, and is described as strong, fierce, voracious, and formidable, not only to fish, which it devours by tribes, but even to men who go into the water near it. It leaps or darts equal to the flight of a bird in rapidity. It has a long, round, and pointed mouth, thick set with sharp teeth; its body is covered with scales of such a texture as to be impenetrable by a rifle bullet, and, when dry, to elicit sparks of fire when struck against steel. It often weighs 200 lbs., and is considered as a far more formidable creature than the alligator, being, in short, the shark of the river, and is as voracious as the shark of the ocean. We saw the body of one of these creatures in the museum of the National Academy of Sciences at St. Louis; and it corresponded in most particulars with the previous description which is given by Hinton, but we could not succeed in seeing one alive. The Devil-jack-diamond fish, or litholepis adamantinus, is another of these river monsters, which is as voracious as the alligator-gar, and like it, has scales which, when dry, will strike fire with steel. It is found from 4 to 10 feet in length; and one has been caught weighing upwards of 400 lbs.

Thus it is clear that great tellers of tall tales were not confined to America.

✱ ✱ ✱ ✱

Few persons, at least among those of the older generation, have not read that classic tale of American humor, "Pigs is Pigs." Mr. Butler's fishing story may not be as well known.

THE REFORMATION OF UNCLE BILLY
Ellis Parker Butler
from the Century Magazine, February 1899

"Lyin' is lyin', be it about fish or money," remarked the deacon, dogmatically, "an' is forbid by Scripter, an' he can't be saved an' freed from sin till he does stop lyin'. That's all there is to it. Billy Matison's got to give up fish-lyin', or he won't never git into the kingdom."

"Well, I reckon you're right, deacon," said Ephraim; "but it ought to be some excuse for Billy that he don't harm no one by his lyin'. Seems to me a lie ain't rightly a lie unless it ketches somebody. Ef you lie about a hoss you're tradin', I'll admit that's wrong, 'cause you'd do the other feller dirt; but Billy's lyin' don't fool nobody, an' it don't cost nobody nothin'. An' then you'd ought to be easy on him, seein' how long he's been at it. Why, Billy Matison's been lyin' 'bout fish off an' on for nigh sixty-six year, an' reg'lar, summer an' winter, for the hull time, at that. Now I leave it to you, deacon; it ain't easy to break off short."

They were sitting front of the grocery. All were gray-haired men nearing the end of their lives, and all were members of the First Church. So was Billy, but his one sin cast a doubt in the minds of his friends regarding his salvation. Billy did not worry in the least. His regular daily occupation was to fish from the bridge across the river, and there he would sit day after day, catching nothing, or at least very little. But in the evening, among his cronies before the grocery, he told marvelous tales of the fish he had almost landed, of the big bass he had caught; and when the fishing season ended, and the rendezvous was the stove in the grocery, all these tales were retold, while it was observed that they had grown strangely during their period of desuetude.

Billy was such a genial, whole-souled liar about his fish that no one had ever had the heart to suggest the improbability of his tales; but a revival had taken place in the village, and under the fervid words of the evangelist the old men had been brought to a full realization of not only their own, but Billy's sins; and the deacon had resolved that Billy must be saved in spite of himself.

"No," admitted the deacon; "it ain't easy to break off short, but it's got to be done. Billy's got to be saved. We know his sin, ef he don't, an' knowin' a sin an' not doin' our best to stop it 'mounts to the same as ef it was our sin, an' I ain't goin' to everlastin' fire jest because Billy Matison lies about the fish he don't ketch."

"That sentiment does you proud, deacon," said Hiram, a weak-eyed old man with a thin, white goatee; "you do yourself proud. That's lovin' your neighbor as yourself."

The deacon felt the delicate flattery, and puffed his pipe in silence a moment, lest he seem puffed up by the compliment.

"Billy Matison has got to be brung up short," he said, at length; "he's gittin' old, an' no tellin' when he will drop off. He's got to be cured now an' at once."

Ephraim had been thoughtfully pushing killikinick into his brier with his thumb. He struck a match on his trousers and puffed the tobacco into a glow.

The deacon opened his mouth again. "Billy Matison has — " he said.

"It's a pity," said Ephraim, interrupting him, "We can't let him break off gradual. When you come to think how long Billy has told fish lies, it seems like the shock of quittin' right sudden might be too much for him — might make him sick or kill him mebby. Now, if he could sort o' taper off like, — say, ketch one less fish a day for a week, or drop off half an inch a day from the size, — it might let him down easy an not try his constitution so bad."

"I would be easier on Billy," said Hiram. The deacon thought deeply for a minute.

"Jest so," he said; "mebby it might strain him to give up all his lyin' at one time, seein' he takes so much pride in it, an' mebby we ought to be a leetle easy on him. Ef Billy Matison was a young feller it would be best, but we can't risk his dyin' unsaved. No; we got to git him to give it up right now. Now is the app'inted time."

"It'll be mortal hard on Billy, come winter," said Amos. "I 'low Billy won't know how to spend the winter ef he can't lie some."

Hiram shook his head sadly.

"I doubt," he said, "ef Billy can live out the winter ef he don't lie. Fish-lyin's got to be all he does winters."

The deacon had been thinking again, and did not catch this remark.

"There's one p'int we must be careful on," he said: "Billy's almight touchy an' we mustn't let on we think he's lyin'. You know how touchy he is, Hiram."

"Thasso," said Hiram. "We can't let on we think he's lyin', he's so dum touchy. Ef we let on he was lyin', an' that we knew he was lyin', he'd go off mad an' never come nigh us."

"An' then we would have a harder job, a big sight, to cure him," said the deacon.

"But I don't see how we can git at him airy other way," said Amos, "for ef we don't let on we know he's lyin' we can't tell him not to lie no more."

"They's jest one way to do it," said the deacon, "an that' the way it's got to be did. We got to make him take back what he lies. Ef he lies an' says he caught a big one, we got to make him tell the truth, an' we got to do it gentle, an' not let on he's lyin'. We got to —"

Here the conversation paused, for around the livery-stable corner came Billy Matison, his fishing-pole slung over his shoulder, his bait and lunch-bucket slung on the pole, and his cane in his hand. As he approached the group of old men, Billy did not appear a very energetic fisherman. His back was bent far forward, and his hand trembled as it held the pole. His cane was a necessity, and not an ornament. His wrinkled face was small, and appeared still smaller under the great home-made straw hat that rested on his long, gray hair. He was an inoffensive, pale-eyed old man, and his toothless gums grasped a blackened clay pipe. Water stood in his eyes. Billy was seventy-eight, and "showed his age."

As he neared the group of old men, they arose. They were but little younger than Billy, and leaned on their canes for support. The straightest of them did not assume the perpendicular at once, but opened gradually from his stooping position, as if his joints had long had the rust of rheumatism.

Billy tottered up to them, unsuspicious of their plot for the safety of his soul. When he reached them, he tremblingly swung his pole and basket to the walk, and sank on the plank bench with a sigh of relief.

Then he took his pipe from his mouth, and holding it out in his shaking hand for emphasis, said in his wavering voice:

"Deacon, I ketched the biggest bass I ever see today. I'll warrant it goes four pound."

Amos glanced at Hiram with pity in his eyes. Of all Billy's lies this was the greatest. But the deacon seated himself beside the fisherman, and putting one hand on Billy's shoulder, said:

"Billy, you an' me has knowed each other forty year, an' in all them years we been good friends, ain't we?"

Billy turned slowly and gazed at the deacon. His lower jaw dropped weakly, as was its wont when he was surprised. Words failed him.

"Ain't we?" insisted the deacon.

Billy replaced his pipe between his lips, and said simply, "Yes."

"An' you recollect how I helped you when you was courtin' 'Manthy? You'd never a' got her but for me, Billy."

Billy's head shook a slow negative.

"An' how I lent you money to build a new house when yourn burned?"

Billy nodded. His eyes sought the faces of the group, but they were stern, and he could fathom nothing there.

"Billy," continued the deacon, "I'm goin' to ask a favor of you. It ain't much. Won't you say that mebby that bass only weighs three pounds an' a half?"

"Well, mebby it does," Billy admitted. "Say three pounds? That bass —" began Billy, but the deacon interrupted him:

"For old friendship's sake, Billy. It's a special favor."

A few more lines gathered in Billy's brow, but he nodded.

"Billy," said the deacon, "you remember the night I brought your boy Jim home when he got lost? Can't you make it two pounds for that?"

Billy gazed doggedly at the plank walk. It was a hard struggle, but he nodded.

"You remember Gettysburg, Billy, an' how I carried you two mile? Can't you make it one pound for Gettysburg?

Billy got up. He was trembling with something besides age now. It was anger.

"Deacon, you mean I'm lyin' — "

"No, Billy," said the deacon, soothingly; "I don't. Mebbe me an' Hiram's got a bet up. Gettysburg, Billy! Make it a pound for me an' Gettysburg."

Billy leaned on his stick with both hands. "It's — a — pound," he said.

"An' now, Billy," the deacon, laying his hand on Billy's arm, while the old men gathered closer about him, "you remember when your Mary Ann went — when she — she left home, an' you — when she visited us until you wanted her back? For that, Billy won't you make it no fish at all? Won't you say you didn't ketch no fish at all to-day, Billy?"

Billy straightened up, and two large drops rolled from his eyes down the gutters of his cheeks.

"Deacon," he said, "I wouldn't do it for no one but you, but for you an' Mary Ann I didn't ketch no fish to-day."

For only one moment the deacon stood triumphant. Then each of the old men grasped Billy's hand firmly, and trudged away, leaving Billy alone, wrapped up in his thoughts. The deacon and Hiram went away together, and the deacon said, "Hiram. It's begun." That was enough.

And Billy! Half stunned, he stood gazing after them. He knew it all. He knew these old friends of his thought him a liar, and that they were trying to save him. Perhaps he should not have yielded, but the deacon had certainly been his best friend, and —

A known liar! A notorious liar!

He picked up his basket with a sigh and slipped it from the pole. Then he painfully mounted the two steps into the grocery.

"Billings," he said, as he placed the basket on the counter and raised the lid, "I ketched a big bass to-day; want you to weigh it."

Billings took the fish from the basket and dropped it into the tin scoop, where it fell with a slap. He pushed the weight along until the beam swayed evenly.

"Four pound, two ounces," he said.

His mouth ain't no prayer book: A teller of gentle lies, as, "Sure, he exaggerates. *His mouth ain't no prayer book.*"

There is a wonderfully colorful southwestern phrase that every busy person will understand, especially those who are so loaded down with responsibility that they shudder at the thought of more. The saying: "I've got more fish now than I can string!"

* * * *

The wife was discussing with a neighbor the previous day's fishing experience with her husband. "I made every mistake in the book!" she said. "I talked too loud. I used the wrong bait! I talked too much, and I reeled in too soon. And to make matters even worse...I caught more than he did!"

* * * *

Grinnin' like a jackass eatin' briars: Real pleased with oneself, as, "Here comes Eddie with a humongous string of bass, and he's *grinnin' like a jackass eatin' briars.*"

* * * *

A wise man, Tony Won, said back in the thirties: "Bait your hook with a bit of vanity and there is not a son of Adam who will not, at least, nibble and mouth it if he doesn't swallow it whole."

* * * *

And that superb magazine of country life, COUNTRY PEOPLE, offered its readers this bit of wisdom: "Take your boy fishing and you won't have to hunt for him."

* * * *

Those Spring drenchers that come on so hard and fast as to leave a fisherman speechless or, at least, powerless to describe them, need be so no longer. You might say, "This rain is sure a goose drownder!" Or, "Man this rain is a pure toad strangler!"

Back in 1926, FARM MAGAZINE printed this cute one.

A strange object was dangling near the young catfish's head.

"What is that thing?" asked his mother, who was nearsighted.

"I'll bite," said the young catfish.

So somebody had fish for breakfast.

* * * *

In a Michigan fishing camp, Pete Brown of Chicago was served a pitcher of orange juice whose flavor was simply superb. He asked the guide where he bought the oranges, and the guide replied that he got them at the "little store just down the road."

So Pete Brown went to that store and bought an entire crate of those oranges, went back to Chicago, took six oranges, squeezed the juice from them, drank and was enormously disappointed. He went to the phone and called the guide up at the camp in Michigan. "Those oranges made a juice not at all like the juice you served. I don't understand it. What do you think?" Pete asked the guide.

"Tell me, Mr. Brown," the guide asked, "What kind of gin did you use with them?"

* * * *

A fellow returned to the office after a fishing trip. He was telling the office staff about the size of one fish that he had almost caught. "I'll bet it was almost as big as a whale," jeered the boss.

"A whale?" replied the fisherman. "Man, I was using a whale for bait!"

* * * *

There was this new-at-it and simple fisherman who was just about half a pint short of a quart! He wanted to go ice fishing, so he asked his buddy if he could borrow his chain saw. He got it and went to the frozen lake. He used the saw for three days! Finally, his neighbor asked for the saw.

But the short-of-brains guy replied, "I ain't done with it, man, I been sawin' and sawin' but I ain't yet got a hole big enough to put my boat in."

* * * *

Here's wisdom: "If you are too busy to go fishing...you're too busy!"

* * * *

FIGS AND THISTLES
Gathered by O.G. Whizz
Printed in FARM LIFE. 1926.

There is no doubt about fishing being an ancient and honorable sport. Long before our savage ancestors devised bows and arrows to shoot game, they fished with bone hooks. We find such hooks today in caves where our great-great-grand-dads-and-mas lived thousands of years ago — ages before Abraham had cut his first teeth or Babylon was even a crossroad village.

How those people ever actually caught fish with such hooks, is a dark and bloody mystery to me. I can hardly do it with the steel ones that we have now. I only get an occasional fish that is low in his mind and reckless, as a result of having been harassed by hordes of other fishermen with their tin minnows and their insane-looking flies made out of peacock feathers and the like. After a fish has bitten into those things a few times and found that they taste like a mixture of neuralgia and lightning, he naturally becomes pessimistic. He mopes around, full of bitter views on life, and in a mood to snap at anything — and so is ripe to be harvested by even as poor a fisherman as myself.

With a bone hook, I would stand about as much show of catching fish as a cow would of successfully jiggling on a slack wire. In fact, I doubt that fish ever were caught on such hooks. Like as not it was the long fruitless attempts to do so that made our far-off ancestors such blood-thirsty savages. You can't tell me that any man could remain calm and sweet-mannered, if he was digging bait day after day, only to see the fish snatch it off one of those bone hooks and caper gleefully off with it; wriggling their noses at him as they went. A thing like that would undermine and corrupt the most angelic disposition. The more I think of it the surer I am that here was the main reason why our cave-dwelling ancestors were so given to pulping each other up.

These reflections are the outcome of a fishing trip that I recently made with the editor and a friend of his, known as "the Deacon." We got 32 bass and crappie, in four days. I caught one-thirty-second of these myself — a solitary bass that died of grief and shame when he saw what kind of a fisherman had got him. The editor was the champion, and you should have seen him sitting in the bow of the boat, using five rods at a time. The Deacon and I, who operated one apiece, were suffering to see him hook about three large, spry bass all at once.

The editor is not an excitable man, but an even-tempered philosopher. Nevertheless, the Deacon and I were all set to get ashore in water ten feet too deep for wading, if three of his flats suddenly went under. But no such joy was vouchsafed us. We could only kid the editor about his five rods, while he smiled the smile of a man whose methods are buttressed with good works.

Finally, when the Deacon had just finished telling him that he ought to get a lot of buggy-whip holders off old carriage dash-boards and festoon them along the sides of the boat to hold his numerous rods, the Editor hooked and landed an especially noble bass.

The Deacon gazed at it sorrowfully for a moment, and then flung his principles overboard. Reaching for two other rods that we had for spares, he said:

"It's no use being bigoted — I'm going to be a two-gun man, myself."

Josh Billings declared, "Enny man who kan swop horses, or ketch fish, and not lie about it, is just about as pious az men ever git to be in this world."

❋   ❋   ❋   ❋

There are more fish taken out of a stream than ever were in it.

— Oliver Herford.

❋   ❋   ❋   ❋

If fish landed were as big as stories told about them, sardines would have to be packed and sold in garbage cans!

❋   ❋   ❋   ❋

The HONEST ABE CLUB was founded as a public service by that superb sportmen's magazine, ARGOSY. To join this prestigious club, subscribers submitted tall tales, that most artful of literary forms, and these, if published, qualified the person for membership. We offer here, a few of the "wisdom tales" submitted and published by ARGOSY MAGAZINE, and reprinted by permission of Argosy Communications. Copyright 1990. All Rights Reserved.

❋   ❋   ❋   ❋

"While fishing with my brother on Chesapeake Bay one day last summer, using his twenty-four-foot cruiser, we noticed that a storm was coming up fast. Using the good sense we had, we decided that we should start for shore some ten miles away.

"We hated to leave, as the fishing was real good that day. Along with the many striped bass that we caught were two really nice-sized dogfish, and the catfish had just started to bite.

"In order to make shore safely, we stopped fishing and revved up the engine to make the return trip, only to find that we had run out of fuel.

"Not being the seaman that my brother is, I became alarmed, but he just sat and studied the situation for a bit and then told me what to do.

"First, I was to catch six large catfish. This I did and left them on long lines as per his instructions. While I was doing this, he started mouth-to-gill artificial respiration on the two big dogfish, and after a short period, he had revived them both to a point where they were growling and barking, just as frisky as could be.

"We then tied the six catfish to the point of the bow and put the two dogfish on heavy lines attached to our strongest rods, and each of us held one on either side of the boat and dropped them in the water.

"As you can imagine, when those dogfish saw the catfish, and vice versa, the race was on. The catfish tried to get away from the dogfish, all the time pulling the boat at a faster speed, with those aggressive dogfish in hot pursuit.

"By close co-ordination and good manipulation of the rods with the dogfish attached, we could guide the catfish in the direction we wanted, and as a result, we beat the storm by a good twenty minutes. There was only some slight damage to the hull of the boat when we went up on the beach, but at least it was on good high ground during the most severe storm of the season.

"Naturally, we turned all the helpful fish loose as a reward for saving us from certain danger. In fact, we turned the catfish loose well in advance of the dogfish to give them a sporting chance."

— Earl F. Linebaugh

✳   ✳   ✳   ✳

Stephen Wiercinski of Ironwood, Michigan, really discovered how to catch worms without even trying:

"Having roamed the north woods since I was knee-high to a chipmunk, which is some sixty-odd years, I am as strong as a bear and as agile as a deer. I can hunt and fish all day and pick night crawlers all night and have never had a serious problem in my life — that is till a couple of months ago. And that's what I want to tell you about and how I licked it.

"The problem was, I couldn't catch night crawlers anymore. I'd spot one and make a grab for it, and it wouldn't be where I grabbed. I had the Doc fix me with a pair of specs and still I missed. Night after night, I would return to the cabin with an empty tin can. Never had I experienced such agony. I tried fishing with plugs and dry flies and got no results. The fish in my lake were just too shrewd to be caught on artificial bait.

"Then one morning, as I sat brooding at my cabin window, my attention was drawn to an old crow that had been hanging around my lawn for a good many years. I had never paid any mind, but believe me, as it came to me now what he was doing, my mind and heart started to perk up and a plan began to rise.

"I tossed and turned in my bunk all night and was up before daybreak, stationed at the window. The old ticker started to pump as the old man crow glided onto the lawn. I watched him pluck a night crawler and lay it aside. Then he plucked another and laid it with the first. Then another.

"It was now time for me to make my play. I leaped to my feet, raced across the floor, jerked open the cabin door and slammed it so hard, it came off the hinges — who cared: my plan had worked. The noise from slamming the door had scared old man crow so bad, he took off for a tall tree like he had jets in his tail section. Brother, if you've ever been cussed out in crow talk, you can imagine the abuse that crow heaped on me as I gathered his cache of worms.

"Well, sir, I had prime bait that day and, as it turned out, every day since, as old man crow still ain't caught on. But best of all, I can now sleep past dawn every morning because I have trained my pet raccoon to get up before old man crow leaves and then slam the door and gather the worms the crow has piled up. However, I think I am going to have to give my raccoon a vacation, as he has taken to shaking like a leaf every time he hears a crow caw. I reckon that crow's abusive language would get to anyone after a spell.

"What I have set down here is the unvarnished truth, and if anyone disbelieves me, they are welcome to come out to my cabin and spell my raccoon — that is, if their souls can take that old crow's abuse."

— Wilbur Neverlye

" BAIT ?... WHAT'S BAIT ? "

Fishermen are probably less confused than most sporting folks. But there does come, if rarely, a sense of just-what-in-the-hell-am-I-doing, by golly! No honest fisherman denies that there are such times. Two artful anglers, Henry Beard and Roy McKie, in their excellent "dictionary", FISHING, published by Workman Publishing Co., New York, 1983, have given us words and their definition that will ease the fishing ways of almost every fisherman. Here are just a few of their fishin' words with meanings that will astound you (and add rods of understanding to your fishing days).

ANGLING: The art of fishing, as practiced by those who seek to catch fish not for profit or for food, but rather for the sport involved. The commonly accepted source of the term "angling" is an ancient Indo-European word, *anka*, meaning "hook" or "to fish with a hook," but several other words are also likely candidates, including *enka* ("unwise expenditure" or "useless task"); *unglo* ("one who is tormented by insects"); *onku* ("loud or frequent lamentation"); *angi* ("to deceive"); *inkla* ("to repeat a foolish act"); *onklo* ("possession by demons"); and *angla* ("love of pointless suffering").

BUCKET: Clumsy form of metallic footgear found on fishing boats.

CLUB: 1. Long bar of wood used to render fish senseless. 2. Place with a long bar of wood where fishermen go to render themselves senseless.

FISHING TRIP: Journey undertaken by one or more anglers to a place where no one can remember when it has rained so much.

LURE: Anything used to attract fish. There are basically two kinds: those fishermen swear by, and those they swear at.

OAR: Clumsy wooden implement used to moisten boat occupants.

RECORDS: The names of current holders of records for game fish are widely published in fishing journals, but individuals who have set new marks in other categories of angling often go unsung. This seems a bit unfair, and it is hoped that this short list will go a long way toward rectifying the more serious omissions:

Tire: 1965, Lake Ontario, 51 1/2 pounds, 35 inches in diameter, Mr. Edward T. Rutherford.

Boot: 1971, Boston Harbor, 7 1/4 pounds, size 11, Mr. Vincent Castelli.

Obstruction: 1958, Santee Reservoir, cypress stump, 36 pounds, 22 inches, Mr. Billy Connors.

Jetsam, Fresh-Water: 1976, Colorado River, G.E. Toaster, 11 pounds, 28 inches (to tip of electric cord), Mrs. Alice Leighton.

Jetsam, Salt-Water: 1960, Pebble Beach, golf club bag with clubs, 38 1/4 pounds, 44 inches, Mr. Thomas P. Landsdowne.

SOLITUDE: The state of being closer to nature than to the nearest flush toilet.

TIPPLING: Method of night fishing in which each cast is followed by a short pull or tug on a bottle held in the free hand. This can lead to erratic casting, but it has the advantage that after a fairly brief period, fish are caught two at a time.

WADING: The most common means through which a dry-fly fisherman is transformed into a wet fly fisherman.

✳ ✳ ✳ ✳

THE MEASUREMENT OF FISH

The more one fishes, and the more one talks about fishing — and what fisherman worth the name does not talk about fishing? — the more it becomes evident that the layman regards the average angler as a person addicted to the most inordinate exaggeration, bordering on positive prevarication, when it comes to referring to the size of the fish he has caught and, more especially, to the size of the fish he has NOT caught.

Such a view is, we need hardly say, entirely false, and is just the sort of thing you would expect from a layman, who knows nothing of the sufferings that have to be borne by the angler in search of his sport.

Considerable fun

The measurement of the fish

MATHEMATICAL ACCURACY UNNECESSARY

After all, an angler does not set himself up as an observer of finicky detail any more than does the golfer or the motorist or the politician. Half a pound more or less here and there, what is it? Such weights as he quotes must be taken as rough estimates, VERY rough estimates, and not as precise measurements to three places of decimals.

Where he tells you that "a pounder rose to my fly in Dingly's Pool," all he means is that a fish of respectable proportions was guilty of this action. If complete accuracy is to be insisted on, conversation about fishing will become even more tedious than it is at the present moment.

The fish he has not caught

HEARTLESS RIDICULE

Then, again, considerable fun is poked at the angler on account of the size of the fish that get away, as quoted by the angler himself.

But is it not after all natural that it will tend to be the big ones rather than the small ones that get away, since they are stronger and more experienced? Of course it will. Hence, the very fact that a fish escapes us in spite of our own vast experience, our considerable skill (if we may make so bold), and our excellent equipment, this very fact, I say, is enough to convince us the fish that gets away must be a large one, possibly a VERY large one, or it would never have contrived successfully to combat the many factors calculated to make such escape impossible. And is it not only natural that the angler, in recounting this dreary affair to a circle of bored listeners in the bar of the local club, should attempt to assess the probable weight, even if roughly, of this cunning creature? Why, of course it is. "It was a couple of pounds if it was an ounce!" he will claim. And who shall say him nay? Who is a better judge of the conceivable avoirdupois of that scaly beauty than the man who, alone and regardless of all personal danger, fought the brute in that deserted spot over the hills, far away from all human succor, until, faint with exhaustion and weakened by the relentless struggle againstunequal odds, he was at long last forced into letting his line go slack for a moment, thus giving the heartless monster the opportunity for which it had been waiting for the last two hours?

No one.

Therefore, let not the enthusiastic beginner be in any way discouraged by the incredulous sneers and vulgar ridicule of those who may attempt to belittle the gallant efforts of our brave anglers, but, confident in the nobility of his cause, tell them to go and boil themselves.

From: CALLING ALL FLY-FISHERS — Alan D'Egville.
David McKay Co. Philadelphia, PA. 1949

Regardless of all personal danger

Ugly: In a bad temper. "Old man Peters began to fish in my area. Didn't even ask, just did. Now that made me some *ugly*."

* * * *

When it comes to tall tales, the champion at this art form must be Vance Randolph whose indefatigable efforts at collecting folklore in the Ozarks resulted in superb compilations of tall tales, that most American of stories. Incidentally, his collections offer insight to the American mind and patterns of behavior. Consider the following four stories from WE ALWAYS LIE TO STRANGERS.

Vance Randolph. Columbia University Press. New York. 1951

* * * *

My friend Jim Haley, at Hot Springs, Arkansas, told me another yarn about a big redhorse. Two giggers sighted the monster in White River near Batesville, Arkansas, and chased it all the way through northern Arkansas, finally making the kill in the James River below Cape Fair, Missouri. That is a hell of a long way by water, and it took most of the summer to make the trip. When the boys were asked how they knew it was the same fish, they answered that there could be no doubt of its identity, because it was still sweating from the long journey when they stuck the gig into it at Cape Fair.

Seldom: A remarkable quality, as, "There's something *seldom* about that trout."

* * * *

A big book could be written about the attempts of Jerry English, well-known Osage River boatman, to catch Old Blue. Since the big dam was built at Bagnell, in 1930, Old Blue spends most of his time in the Lake of the Ozarks, where his doings are reported by "Skunk Hide" Turner and M.N. White, of Warsaw, Missouri. Old Blue has been known to help a trapper by retrieving his lost rabbit-guns and by killing a prime black mink in an unprintable fashion. Once, he jumped over the Bagnell Dam and traveled all the way to Louisville on an errand for one of his friends. Another time, knowing that a big flood was on the way, he put his great tail under a boatman's shanty and moved it up on higher ground. "He done it so gentle like," said the riverman, "that my greasin'-skillet didn't even fall off its peg." Only a few years ago, according to the weekly Kansas City Star, Old Blue stuck his head out of the water and winked his left eye, a movement which caused such a rush of wind that a big elm tree was torn loose from its roots and blown into the river.

Old Blue has been hooked many times, but landed only once — and perhaps it wasn't really Old Blue that time. The story is that a fellow named Reeves caught a catfish so God-awful big that the lake fell fourteen feet when he dragged it out. Hundreds of launches and sailboats were stranded high and dry, and lakeside cottagers awoke to find half-a-mile of mud between their cabins and the water. Seeing the whole future of the summer-resort business in danger, local business men finally prevailed upon Reeves to return his prize to the water, whereupon the lake became normal. "I shore did hate to throw that there fish back," sighed the fisherman.

* * * *

Take a fit: To do something on impulse, as, "I *took a fit* to buy me a fly-fishin' outfit and learn how to do it."

I have heard several tales about dogs which are of great assistance to fishermen. It is said that Cleo Bilberry, of Smithville, Arkansas, used to have a pair of shepherd dogs trained to catch bass. The Springfield, Missouri Leader and Press, tells of one occasion when the dogs bark treed down by the creek. They had cornered a whole school of bass in a narrow pool, and Bilberry had no trouble in catching a nice string while the dogs prevented the fish from escaping.

A boatman at Oceola, Missouri, swears that he used to own a trained fish-dog which could catch more bass than any two fishermen in the state. The animal wore a specially designed harness, to which a number of lines and trolling-spoons were attached. Sent into the water, he swam about until several fish had hooked themselves, and then returned to his master who stood waiting on the dock. Several times the dog was pulled under by the sheer weight of bass, and once the owner had to dive under a raft to rescue him from a twenty-pound jack salmon. Yessiree Bob!

* * * *

Marinator: A herring aide.

* * * *

Another fisherman, in casting out, lost his watch. But he continued fishing for some time, and actually caught a five-pounder, a bass. But when he noticed the anguish, the appealing look in the fish's eyes, this nice guy threw the fish back.

Now, consider that the next time that fisherman fished that very same fishin' hole, at least a year later, he saw a bass circling his boat in a way that seemed strange. He looked closely and saw that the bass had a watch in his mouth and seemed to want the fisherman to take it. Turned out to be the very same watch he'd lost. Yep! Talk about casting bread upon the waters! Or is it watches?

But that's not all. The watch was running. That grateful fish had wound that watch every day for a year. And it was only a few minutes slow.

"Unfortunately, we got hungry on the way back with this one."

Upstream, Downstream and Out of My Mind. Syd Hoff. © 1961

Bun in the oven: "Jake can't go fishin' for awhile. His missus has got a *bun in the oven*." (She's pregnant!)

✳   ✳   ✳   ✳

Faht: Fastidious, prissy, as, "What an old *faht* he is, wears a necktie while trout-fishin'." (New England)

✳   ✳   ✳   ✳

There are many American fishermen who lack "smarts" about fishing. Such would profit from a careful study of the ways to catch fish. Most know about worms on the hook or minnows or artificial plugs, flies, spinners and the like, but there are many more baits and lures to help fill the frying pan. We'll reveal a few of them below, so *vide* (Latin for take-a-peek).

＊ ＊ ＊ ＊

Mystical is the use of sleeping pills for bait. Yes, there are fishermen who bait with them. This one savvy guy came back with a string of walleyes you wouldn't believe. "How'd you catch 'em? What kind of bait?" he was asked.

Direct and honest as all fishermen are, he replied, "Sleeping pills. I laced the water with a bottle of 'em and when the fish rises to yawn, well, I stick a hook in his mouth and reel him in." Such are called pharmaceutical fishermen.

Now the mechanical-minded fisherman is of a different type. Consider Ezekial Phil. He was such a man. He would arise early, before daybreak, go out on his boat to the fishing hole, then let his alarm clock ring. "When the fish rise in anger to turn off the alarm, Ezekial just hits 'em over the head with a ball bat. Voila! Fresh fish for breakfast."

The unique method developed by Ezekial Phil can be put to a similar use. When the ice is frozen, you cut a small hole in it, then hold your thermometer over it and, when the fish rise to detect the temperature, you render the *coup de grace* with the bat!

＊ ＊ ＊ ＊

Strike up with: To meet, as, "It's a pleasure to *strike up with* a feller who enjoys fly-fishin'."

＊ ＊ ＊ ＊

Tall tales are not the exclusive province of country folks sitting around the stove at the local store. This one was told by George Swier, head of the Bloomington, Illinois, Water Department. He was telling the reporter, for the ILLINOIS STATE JOURNAL of Springfield, Illinois, about the horrendous drought that threatened to ruin the water supply of Bloomington. It seems that the two lakes that supply water were now no more than shallow ponds. He went on to explain, "Somebody did catch the world's record catfish up at Lake Bloomington, the other day. They used two gallons of water for bait!" Now that's so-o-me drought!

* * * *

Then there's the verified story about the fellow who hooked a big carp in early morning. He worked the live-long day to pull that fish in. Finally, at the end of the day, he tied the line to a huge oak stump and went home to sleep. The next day he tried again, but couldn't pull the fish to shore. After three days he managed to horse the huge fish up on the bank. He dragged the blamed fish toward home, but it weighed so much it sunk a channel in the cement road!

He tried to kill that fish, but it was too large. So he kept it alive in an enormous water tank, handily placed so that he could cut fillets from the fish as he wanted them. After many months of good eating, his company ordered him to New York City, and he was forced to give the fish to a nearby family. The lady of the house wrote to keep him informed about the cooperative, obliging fish. She wrote that she was slicing in to where the fillets were "jest dandy." She mentioned that the carp often asked about his welfare.

* * * *

Dub around: To putter, dawdle, as, "Joe likes to *dub around* with his flyrod. But he don't ketch nothin'." (New England)

Almost everybody has heard of fellows who actually can "witch" for water, using a forked stick that turns downward no matter how firmly held, when the well-witcher moves over a supply of underground water suitable for a liberal supply of well-water. Well, there are some men who can use the same inborn skill to find fish. Take a look at this story:

"I got up one morning and decided to go fishing. I went to the lake and set down on the bank and baited my hook and threw it into the water and waited awhile. I hadn't got a bite for awhile when all at once my pole went bending and pointing and pointing up the lake. It kept on pointing up the lake, so I went up the lake until it quit pointing and threw my hook in and caught two bass that weighed 3 1/2 pounds a piece. Then it went to pointing up the lake further, so I went up the lake further and threw my hook in, and it hadn't more than hit the water when I got a strike and hung it. It was a 7 pound bass, and I threw my hook out again and caught another 7 pound bass. So I thought that was so good I would go a lot further up the lake. So I went about a quarter of a mile further up the lake and started to throw my hook and my pole started to point back down the lake, but I decided to try it here, but before I could throw my hook in a 200 pound bluegill jumped out on the bank and swallowed me, and if it hadn't been for that pole pointing our way out, I wouldn't be here to tell you about that 21 pounds of bass I caught."

— Larry Maggard

* * * *

Kansas City fish: Bacon.

* * * *

A 12-year-old kid was told to take care of his sister during the time his folks went shopping in town. He went fishing, his little sister with him.

"I'll never, ever do that again, Mom," he told his mother, after returning that night.

"Don't say that, honey," his Mother cautioned, "I'm sure she'll be a good girl and mind you the next time you take her with you."

"Aw, she was good enough, Ma," the kid said, "my only problem with her was that she ate the bait!"

* * * *

It could only have happened in New England! You see, the town Mayor stopped at the bridge to watch a fellow townsman fish.

"Doin' any good, Sam?" the Mayor asked.

"Nope."

"Ain't they biting?"

"Nope."

"You been fishin' long, Sam?"

"Since afore breakfast."

"Well," remarked the mayor, "they can't be many fish where you're afishin' Sam, can there?"

"They ain't," Sam said, "but it's a danged sight better'n no fishin' atall."

* * * *

Most every fisherman has heard about the fellow who caught a whopper, the biggest fish he had ever caught. Well, he took a picture of it just to prove the enormous size. And that picture weighed 4 1/2 pounds! Yep! Well, there's an even more likely story about a man and wife who went fishing in Wyoming. He flipped a feathered dingbat into a likely spot and got a crashing strike! That fish took off with boat, wife, fisherman, hook, line and sinker. But, alas, the fish got away. Fortunately, the wife was an excellent artist. She used the empty paper sack that had held their lunch and drew a picture of that fish. Well, that drawing alone weighed forty pounds. Of course, to be honest, one must deduct the weight of the paper bag!

* * * *

Muckle: To grasp or hold, as, "*Muckle* onto that end of the canoe and I'll lift t'other end."

It was terribly dry in southern Missouri one year and the crappie taken from lakes and rivers were so derned dusty they could not be eaten.

* * * *

A fellow from near Beardstown, Illinois, told this story and he swears that it is true, with evidence to prove it. He was fishing one day and noticed a big grasshopper suspended on a weed overhanging the water. The reflection attracted bass, and they were jumping for that reflection. All the fisherman had to do was cast in the general vicinity of the reflection, and he got bass after bass after bass. He caught six! And when he got home and cleaned the fish, each one contained from eight to 12 grasshopper reflections. And were they fat. From the reflections, no doubt. He says he put all the reflections in a bottle so that if any reader doubts his story, he is invited to the fellow's house and he'll prove it by showing the englassed reflections. Please write the editor for name and address.

* * * *

Vance Randolph dedicated his life to the collection and literary organization of folklore from the Ozark hill country. The following two stories are from his published collection *FUNNY STORIES FROM ARKANSAS.*

Everybody knows that the Northfork River is a mighty lively little stream, and one hears some strange stories about it. One fisherman who made a float-trip there said the current was so damned swift that the water was actually heated by its friction against the rocks. The farther he floated the warmer the water became, until by the time they got to Henderson Ferry the water was fairly steaming, and the bottom of the boat so hot that it blistered his feet, right through his horse-hide moccasins. When he finally left the river at Norfolk, Ark., the fish on his stringer, which had been trailing in the water, were cooked to a turn!

One of my neighbors near Bella Vista, Ark., used to tell of his adventure with a huge catfish in Sugar Creek. This fish had been seen many times, and our best fishermen had tried to catch him. He had broken countless hooks, lines, rods and trotline stagings. Spears and bullets made no impression upon his broad back, and many a gigger's john-boat had been capsized by a contemptuous swing of his mighty tail. And, once, it is said he drowned a poor drunken noodler who was so foolish as to strap the noodle-hook fast to his wrist.

In the Summer of 1928 my neighbor resolved to catch this catfish or perish in the attempt. He had the local blacksmith forge a hook two feet long, and used the well-rope for a line, with two sashweights by way of sinkers. Baiting with a full-grown groundhog, he tied the rope to the top of a stout elm and lowered the hook into the depths of Sugar Creek.

"I was down to the creek afore sunup next mornin'," he told me. "That big ellum-tree was tore plumb out of the ground, with roots ten foot long a-stickin' up in the air!"

"Well, did you catch the fish?" I asked.

"I clumb out on the tree an' got hold of the rope," the fisherman went on calmly. "Then I pulled on the line, slow an' keerful. There was a heavy weight on the other end, but seemed like it was a dead weight — there wasn't no fightin' like I expected. So I just figgered...."

"Did you get the fish?" I shouted.

"Naw," he answered, "I didn't git the fish. But I did git about seventy-five pounds of his upper lip!"

Haldeman-Julius. 1949. Girard, Kansas.

✳   ✳   ✳   ✳

Too wet to plow: The end! Finished! And nothing to do about it, as, "We lost all our gear. From then on it was just *too wet to plow.*"

A reporter traveled to the home of old Joe Barley who was reputed to be the laziest man in the county. The reporter figured there was a good story in Joe. So he talked to him about his work habits while Joe was fishing in the creek, just outside his cabin, an occupation the townspeople said was habitual.

"Do you have a job now?"

"Nope."

"This year or last?"

"Nope."

"Have you ever worked, Joe?"

"Oh sure. You bet. I work every week that ain't got Friday in it."

＊　＊　＊　＊

There is no use in your driving 50 miles to fish when you can depend on being just as unsuccessful near home.

＊　＊　＊　＊

Every fisherman, duck hunter or field trailer has experienced the thunderous snores of a companion asleep after a long day in the field. Ed Zern tells of just such an earsplitting experience and how, sometimes, sound speaks louder than words.

Jim got to reminiscing about a trip we'd taken 10 years ago to a hotel in the Adirondacks near Osgood Pond, where we were fishing for smallmouth bass. Because Jim and I were the only ones in the party without our wives we shared a double room, but Jim snored with such earsplitting, rafter-rattling ferocity that I moved to a single room at the opposite end of the hotel the following day. Jim was a bit ruffled by this, and accused me of exaggerating the volume and vehemence of his log sawing; however, when we met for breakfast the third morning he seemed strangely pensive.

"Maybe you weren't exaggerating," he finally said. "This morning about three o'clock I was awakened by a knocking on my door. When I stumbled over and opened it there was a nice old man standing there. When he saw that I was in pajamas and the room was dark he was surprised, and finally blurted out, 'I'm sorry to trouble you. I just wanted to see what you were building.'"

* * * *

FISHIN' TIME

Oh, you can talk of hunter's cunnin'
And the many sports of gunnin',
And there is a bit of pleasure in the pastime I've no doubt.
But for good and wholesome pleasure
There is nothing that will measure
With the river bank in the springtime, when the trout are
out.

So he takes his hook and line where the dashin'
Little streamlet comes a splashin,
And he tosses in his minnow, settles back and takes a
chew.
Then he does some watchful waitin'
And a lot of skillful baitin',
But what he catches is mighty small and few.

When the evenin' shades are fallin',
And the whip-poor-wills are callin',
You will see him slippin' homeward, nothin' daunted,
spirits gay.
He'll tell you how he hung em.
Lots of big ones too, among em.
But he didn't land so many, all the big ones got away.

Nothin' Ain't No Good. E.P. Holmes.
Clay Printing Co. 1955. Winston Salem, N.C.

HOW TO GO FISHING THOUGH MARRIED

It is becoming increasingly clear to all lovers of fishing that the sport will soon fade from the face of the earth unless drastic measures are taken. Statistics show that the average married man can only go fishing a few times a year. This comes about because of the average wife, who would much rather keep her husband at home mowing the lawn, changing sink washers or beating rugs.

Accordingly, out of my personal passion for the sport, I've devised the following tactics for harassed husbands who yearn for the rapture of piscatorial pleasures:

1: THE VOLUNTEER FIREMAN METHOD

This is a fairly simple way to get out of the house if you happen to live in a small town. The first essential is to contact your local volunteer fireman brigade and enroll at once as a member. Whenever the fishing bug hits, have a friend in the firehouse sound the alarm. When the alarm rings, grab fire fighting equipment in one hand. Grab fishing tackle in the other hand, on way out to garage. (If the alarm rings at night, go night fishing.)

2: THE LITERARY METHOD

This is an excellent system for fishermen with a literary bent. Notify your wife that you are about to write a book about marine life. She will be proud of you at once. Tell her you must make occasional field trips to do research. Now you are free to go fishing whenever you like.

At the end of the season, tell her that your book was rejected by every publisher in the field. Nine out of ten wives will swallow this yarn. The tenth may call you a liar.

If married to the tenth, there's only one way out of the mess. Better write the book.

3: THE FRESH AIR METHOD

This is an easy method for all husbands who happen to be anemic. Begin by complaining about your state of health. Develop a pasty, sallow complexion. To do this, stop eating, drinking and sleeping. After a few weeks of this, the little woman should notice your bony condition.

A visit to the family doctor will gain the required results. A good doctor will advise fishing as an aid for your general health. A friendly wife will follow his advice.

For perfect results, make sure your wife is friendly.

4: THE INFALLIBLE METHOD

Get a divorce.

FISH AND BE DAMNED. Lawrence Lariar 1953.
Prentice-Hall, Inc. New York

Ed Zern is a genius at hunting and fishing humor. And he's been writing it for delighted sportsmen for many years. Many know his "Exit Laughing" column for FIELD & STREAM and there is a list of his books below.

He's written for AUDUBON, TRUE, THE NEW YORK TIMES, SPORTS ILLUSTRATED and others. There's even a rumor that St. Peter is considering, as a requirement for entry, the telling of one Ed Zern fishing or hunting story (this may be idle rumor).

Here is a mere smidgin', a taste of his...literature!

According to my own statistical survey, there are exactly 749,621 people in this country who work fifty weeks a year so that they can afford to go fishing for the other two weeks. And of this number, exactly 749,619 arrive at their favorite stream or lake to find that the water is too high, too low, too muddy, too clear, too cold, too warm, too something or too other for good fishing.

Of the other two people, one slips on a stone and breaks his leg in two places the first day, and the other is so flabbergasted that he upsets the canoe and loses his tackle.

* * * *

The chief difference between big-game fishing and weight-lifting is that weight-lifters never clutter up their library walls with stuffed bar-bells.

I once asked a professional psychologist, "What makes fishermen tick?" He said he would look into it, and after several weeks of intensive research he reported that it was a peculiarity of their skulls. (It seems he had understood me to ask, "What makes fishermen thick?")

There's a rumor that the middle figure, top row, represents Ed Zern. Others say that they couldn't recall that he had freckles. Mr. Zern here presents a gallery of fishermen —type by type.

Unbalanced
Fisherman

Hung-over
Fisherman

Triumphant
Fisherman

Late-Rising
Fisherman

Honest
Fisherman

Purist

Convivial
Fisherman

Night
Fisherman

Skunked
Fisherman

We've seen Ed Zern's analysis of fishermen's feelin's. Here he applies his wisdom to fish-feelin's.

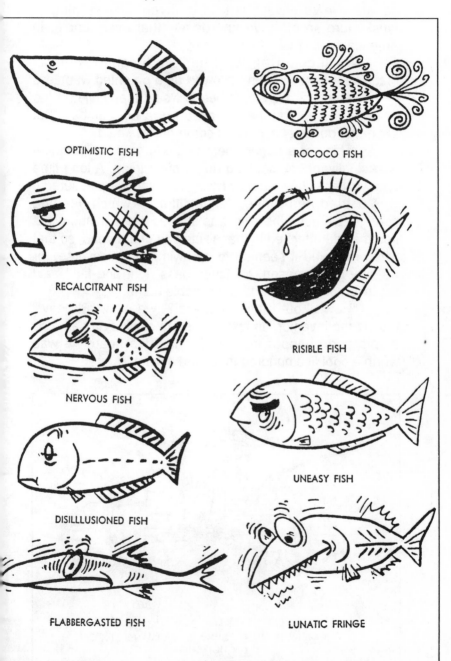

OPTIMISTIC FISH

ROCOCO FISH

RECALCITRANT FISH

RISIBLE FISH

NERVOUS FISH

UNEASY FISH

DISILLLUSIONED FISH

FLABBERGASTED FISH

LUNATIC FRINGE

HOW TO GET RICH QUICK

One of the pleasanter ways to make a million dollars, we've always felt, is to invent a bass plug or musky lure so effective and deadly that every angler in America would rush to lay in a supply.

We thought of this when we lunched with Bill Matthias recently, and he showed us a patented weedless lure invented by his stepfather. Bill said they called it the Allureo, and agreed that it looked like a hot number. "But the name doesn't have much come-on," we said.

"Think of a better one," said Bill, "and we'll change it." Actually, of course, he'd do no such thing. A long time ago we were shown a new bass plug, and were assured it was a tried-and-proved killer-diller — which seemed strange, because the plug was shaped like a minnow, but had the line attached to the tail instead of the head, so that when retrieved it seemed to be swimming in reverse, for no very good reason. "Catches bass right and left," said the inventor. "All it needs is a suitable name."

"How about 'Bass Ackward'?" we said. "Phooey!" replied the inventor, and proceeded to call it by a name so stupid and unappealing that the last we heard he was worth a cool five hundred thousand dollars.

"HEAVEN IS JUST LIKE I ALWAYS HOPED IT WOULD BE."

Mr. Zern was always a great benefactor of the underdog/fish/worm. Here his artistry at underdogging is revealed in all its piscine beauty.

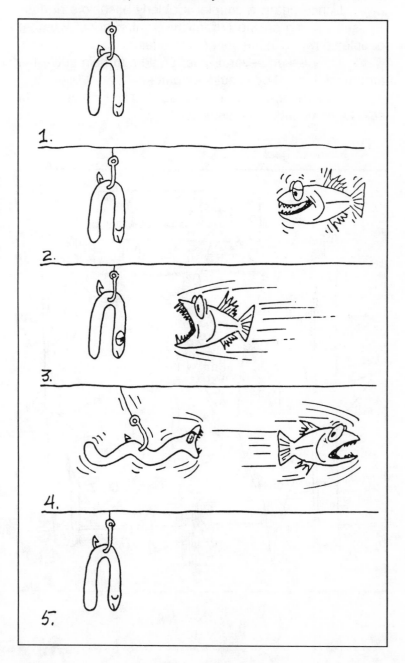

THE SEX LIFE OF FISHERMEN

Most fishermen are completely uninterested in sex. They figure it does not pay to have too many hobbies.

I once heard a couple of elderly bachelors at Jack Russell's camp on the Miramichi arguing about whether people spawned in the spring or the fall.

They asked several other anglers to help settle the argument, but nobody could remember.

In general, fishermen are abysmally ignorant about sex. Or name any other subject.

Mr. Zern is not only a savvy fisherman, but he knows a few things about the intimate lives of his fish, too. Just witness this...

* * * *

THE SEX LIFE OF FISHES

The truth is, fish have very little sex life. If you have ever tried to make love under water, you will know why.

When a boy wall-eyed pike sidles up to a girl wall-eyed pike and tries to say: "Kiddo, you impress me as a very fancy number. You got that certain je ne sais quoi. What are you doing this evening, baby?" it comes out "Glub." This sort of thing is not conducive to successful courtship.

If you tell a bluegill a risque joke, the chances are he won't get it.

According to Jordan and Evermann's American Food and Game Fishes, a single eel will lay 10,000,000 eggs. Presumably a married eel will do just as well, or better.

During the spawning season, male brook trout become highly colored.

Female brook trout think this is cute as the dickens.

BOOKS BY ED ZERN

To Hell with Fishing
To Hell with Hunting
How to Tell Fish from Fishermen
How to Catch Fishermen
Are Fishermen People?
A Fine Kettle of Fish Stories
Hunting and Fishing from A to Zern

Too, Ed Zern is a practical man. He can sure tie knots.

HANDY KNOTS FOR FISHERMEN No. 1

Especially recommended for use on neighbors who say, "Well, I suppose the big one got away again, ha ha!" Also for your aunt, who sold your Uncle Leonard's rod to the junkman for 35¢ when the old boy passed on, and many other uses too numerous to mention.

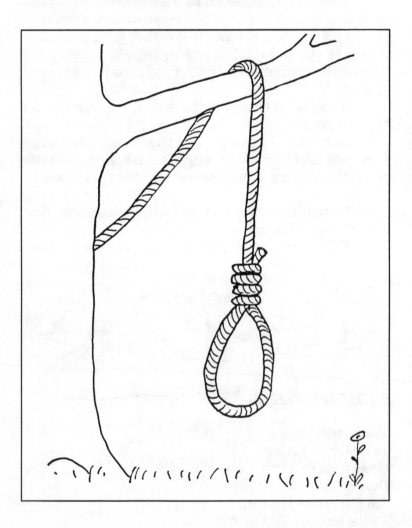

The following tale reminds us of the time when Sunday fishing was a sin! And the sin was engaged then, as now. But back then, the fisherman had to be a tad more cautious, careful, even devious— in 1888!

* * * *

THE TELESCOPE FISH-POLE CANE

There is one thing we want to set our face against and try and break up, and that is the habit of young and middle aged persons going fishing on Sunday, when going on the summer excursions to the country. The devil, or some other inventor, has originated a walking-stick that looks as innocent as a Sunday school teacher, but within it is a roaring lion, in the shape of a fish-pole. We have watched young fellows, and know their tricks. Sunday morning they say to their parents that they have agreed to go over on the West Side and attend early mass with a companion, just to hear the exquisite music, and by the way, they may not be home to dinner. And they go from that home, with their new cane, looking as pious as though they were passing the collection plate. When they get around the corner they whoop it up for the depot, and shortly they are steaming out into the country. They have a lot of angle worms in an envelope in their vest pockets, and a restaurant colored man, who has been seen the night before, meets them at the depot and hands them a basket of sandwiches with a bottle sticking out.

Arriving at the summer resort, they go to the bank of the lake and take a boat ride, and when well out in the lake they begin to unbosom the cane. Taking a plug out of the end of it, they pull out a dingus and three joints of fish-pole come out, and they tie a line on the end, put an angle worm on the hook, and catch fish. That is the kind of "mass" they are attending.

At night the train comes back to town, and the sunburnt young men, with their noses peeled, hand a basket to the waiting colored man, which smells of fish, and they go home and tell their parents they went out to Forest Home Cemetery in the afternoon, and the sun was all hot. The good mother knows she smells fish on her son's clothes, but she thinks it is some new kind of perfumery, and she is silent.

An honest up-and-up fish-pole is a thing of beauty and a joy forever, if the fishing is good, but one of these deceptive, three card monte, political fish-poles, that shoves in and appears to be a cane, is incendiary, and ought to be suppressed. There ought to be a law passed to suppress a fish-pole that passes in polite society for a cane, and in such a moment as ye think not is pulled out to catch fish. There is nothing square about it, and the invention of that blasted stem winding fish-pole is doing more to ruin this country than all the political parties can overcome. If there was a law to compel the owners of those walking-sticks to put a sign on their canes, "This is a fish-pole," there would be less canes taken on these Sunday excursions in summer.

* * * *

If you ever wondered about the power of heredity, let your mind work on these following two examples from both the animal and the fish world, from the *SOUTHERN FOLKLORE QUARTERLY*, December 1944.

THE FISH AND THE FRYING PAN

This actually happened to a fisherman up at Moosehead. He had caught a five-pound trout, and was going to fry it for supper. While it was cooking over the fire, he turned away for a minute to get a plate, and when he looked around, the fish had flopped off with the frying pan, by gorry. Next spring that fisherman caught the same fish, with the frying pan on his tail, and the next five fish he caught all had little frying pans on their tails.

ALL ABOUT ICE FISHING

I was driving through Pike County, Pennsylvania, one particularly cold and blowy January, and stopped off to visit with Gollup Kuhn, the undisputed champeen free-style liar of Lackawaxen. After he'd plied me with ripe cider Gollup suggested that the big pool in Delaware, right in front of his house, was frozen good and thick, and that we might do some ice fishing. Sitting in the warm kitchen it seemed like a fine idea, and we went.

That was the first time I'd ever ice-fished, and if I keep my wits about me it will be the last. Three hours later we were back in the kitchen, and pretty soon I had thawed out enough to notice that Gollup was talking.

Some years ago, Gollup said, a local gent had been ice fishing on the same pool and had stepped on a thin spot and gone through. That was the last anybody had heard of him until the following March, when his wife received a telegram from the Chief of Police of Port Jervis, some twenty miles downriver. The telegram read: "Your husband's body found stop in very bad condition and full of eels stop wire instructions."

The bereaved lady, according to Gollup, hotfooted it down to the depot and sent off the following directive: "Sell eels stop. Sell proceeds stop. Set him again."

* * * *

"The codfish lays ten thousand eggs:
The homely hen lays one.
But the codfish never cackles
To tell you what she's done.
And so we scorn the codfish,
While the humble hen we prize —
Which simply goes to show you
That it pays to advertise!"

SONG TO A CATFISH

To look at a living catfish,
Which is grey, which is whiskered and slick,
You may say, "Nunh-unh, none of that fish,"
And look away quick.
But fried,
That's the sweetest fish you ever tried.
Put a little dough on your hook and throw it out thayor
And pop you got a fish that cooked'll be fit for a mayor.
Closed white fishfleshflakes, wrapped in crunch...
I couldn't eat all the catfish I could eat for dinner if
I started at lunch.

Soupsongs. Roy Blount, Jr. Houghton Mifflin Co., Boston 1957

✳ ✳ ✳ ✳

We end it with yet another view of our biblical
Jonah, of fish, and of fishing stories. By now, dear reader,
we hope that you, too, are hooked on the joy, the fun, the
healthy value of humor, laughter and fishin'.

A STORY OF A WHALE AND A WHALE OF A STORY

This is the first of all fishing stories, and if you can
swallow this, there is no reason for supposing that the
whale did not swallow Jonah.

Jonah was a prophet, who like Elijah went for a
cruise — but not with a widow. The present cruising craze
is not such a novelty as we are led to believe. In Jonah's
time, for instance, there was quite a good cruise running
from Joppa to Tarshish. Even prophets have to have a
holiday sometimes, especially as they get more honor
abroad, so Jonah shipped on board at Joppa.

No sooner was the ship out of sight of land,
however, than a storm came up. Jonah was a good sailor
and, being a prophet, had the additional advantage of
possessing a clear conscience, so he remained sound
asleep down below. The gallant crew were simply stiff with
terror about this storm and finally, the captain, who hated
to see a mere landsman sound asleep and

oblivious of the storm while his crew were having such a bad time of it, came and, shouted out, "Jonah, art thou sleeping there below?" Or words to that effect.

The crew, after a lot of argument and finding no one else on whom they could lay the blame for the storm, decided rather illogically that the storm was all Jonah's fault. "You are a Jonah!" said the captain, and they all agreed that the only solution would be to jettison Jonah. So they did. Whether this was to lighten the craft or whether it was because they were jealous of Jonah's seamanship is not known.

Now that would have been the end of the story, had it not been for the fish world. Just at that moment a whale named Leviathan was swimming by on its way to Whale Island and, believe it or not, it swallowed Jonah, thus preserving him from a watery grave. The whale was probably quite oblivious of the fact that Jonah was a prophet. To a whale a prophet tastes very much the same as a lettercarrier or a member of Congress. So down went Jonah into the whale's interior, wishing he had never gone on that cruise and probably thinking a few un-prophetlike thoughts on the behavior of mariners in general.

It is very fortunate that at this time the reign of Neptune was over, otherwise Jonah might have become a marine deity instead of one of our most popular prophets.

Jonah was in the whale's belly, rocked in the cradle of the deep, for three days and three nights with nothing to live on but superfluous blubber and whale oil. How Jonah calculated the time is not known. We can't prove that he was in there four days or four nights, so there the matter remains — and so did Jonah.

After a while the whale became tired of the foreign body lodged in the duodenum and feeling rather seasick after the storm, it brought Jonah up with a relieved eructation and on to the land in the bargain. This was very sporting of the whale and is just the kind of thing which a nation of fishermen will appreciate. It is a pity that the whale unobtrusively leaves us at this part of the story and we are therefore unable to enhance the value of this history of the fish world with an account of its subsequent career.

Thus the fish world leaves its first mark on the pages of our history. After swallowing that — the story, not Jonah — people would believe anything, so fishing stories became much wilder.

Fishin' Fun. W.A. Brooks. 1954
Derby Press. N.Y.

* * * *

In his home study, President Herbert Hoover hung this prayer, a prayer echoed by every fisherman.

God grant that I may fish
Until my dying day!
And when it comes to my last cast
I humbly pray,
When in God's landing net
I'm peacefully asleep,
That in His mercy I be judged
As good enough to keep.

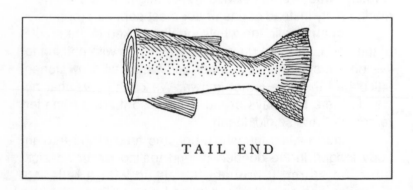

TAIL END

HUNTING SECTION

"I KNOW WE'VE TAUGHT YOU IT'S NOT POLITE TO POINT, SON,... THIS IS DIFFERENT — TRUST ME."

INTRODUCTION

It is impossible to describe to a non-hunter, the pleasure, the pure joy granted the man who tramps the hunter's field, or sits in the hunter's blind, or just sits at home and dreams of the experiences of the last hunt or what might come to him in the future. The non-hunter can understand the fisherman's pleasure because he, too, regularly eats fish, reads of commercial fishermen, sees fish for sale at the super market, and can — if he wishes — keep fish at home in a bowl! To most people, killing fish and eating them is innocent — about like growing tomatoes at home, and eating them.

But the hunter? That's a pup of a different gender...to the person who doesn't hunt. Hunting is...yes, you could say it...a different kettle of fish! You can't buy wild duck, or wild quail, or pheasant, or venison at the super market. Therefore, you can't get adjusted to it so as to consider it benign...as you adjust to catching and killing fish.

So how can you make the non-hunter understand the ineffable beauty of a quail shoot through lovely fall pastures, on an incomparably beautiful day? Or make them visualize the joy in seeing a skein of ducks flowing your way with every chance of a fair shot at them? Or the thrill that comes to you as your pointer or setter freezes on point, then moves to retrieval? Too, the critic cannot sense the woe, the gravity of disappointment when the bird is missed! Or when the dog louses up the point. And all of this on a November day so quiet, so beautiful, so God-blessed that memory forever retains it. Sex you can explain to a non-participant. Possibly. Hunting you cannot! Ever!

Just how does one explain that the sport is not only beautiful and fun, but so exciting that there is no easy sleep the night before the first hunt of the season. As the excited hunter dozes off to sleep, a covey of quail flushes in front of his mind's eye and he jerks around to lay his gun on the bird. He's wide-awake now. And then he must wait, once again, for sleep to come knowing that all of this night he is fated to doze, jerk awake then turn and fire at the birds that are utterly real to his mind's eye only.

You can't explain it. You have to do it! You have to hunt and experience the hunter's game if you would understand the millennial joy that men find in it.

Clearly, there will always be the Esaus that hunt and the Jacobs who stay at home, the pride and joy of their mother's eye. And the Esaus will limit the kill, preserve the game, use every care and caution to maintain the species and have fun with wild game. Every honest hunter knows that conservation makes sense, makes more and better hunting. And THAT hunters understand better than their critics.

Doubtless, Esau told funny stories, too. And enjoyed them. Although there is not much humor in the Bible, still we can be sure that Esau told stories to father Isaac who laughed uproariously and who cherished them as much as the wild game he asked Esau to kill for him. True, Esau got a raw deal. Rebecca "done him wrong". And, doubtless, Esau saw the funny side of that, too, and joked about it over campfires thousands of years ago.

From then until today, the fraternity of hunters (Esauites all), have created some of the world's best humor — jokes, cartoons, stories, sayings, aphorisms — that have been created to reflect the fun of the sport. A selection of the best...follows.

AN IMPROVED TARGET

Here is a target that is certain to please both novice and experienced hunters as well as those with bad eyesight, palsy, unexpected eructations, and awful aim! Now... anyone...anyone at all can hit the bullseye, hence the name, "The Equalizing Bullseye". Package of twenty five......$9.00

Throughout this book there are hunting and fishing stories, folktales, collected by the greatest assembler of Ozark folklore — Vance Randolph. Some of these stories are original to the land and others trace their origins back to the countries of origin, notably, the British Isles. All are not only funny but reveal the superb sense of humor of the frontier American who lived with rude cabins, candlelight, home-procured and butchered meat, home-grown food, privies and...loneliness.

The Ozark country, in the first fifty years of this century, retained the language, ideas, customs and humor of our earliest settlers. Vance Randolph recognized the importance of this cache of folklore and spent years collecting it for posterity. Needless to say, hunting and fishing jokes with laughter, and all kinds of funny stories were, to these fascinating Ozark people, essential to their culture and contentment.

The next several stories are from Vance Randolph's collection, *WE ALWAYS LIE TO STRANGERS, TALL TALES FROM THE OZARKS.* Columbia University Press. 1951. New York, NY

* * * *

It was my impression that the scarcity of wild turkeys is due to the native practice of shooting them in season and out, particularly the killing of fryin'-size poults. But a man named Cummins, who lived on Bear Creek near Walnut Shade, Missouri, set me right about this. He said it was the illegal use of gobble-weed which had well-nigh exterminated the turkeys in his neighborhood. Gobble-weed is obtained from the Cherokees, he said, and consists of dried leaves and berries to be scattered on the ground. As soon as a turkey eats a bit of this stuff, it shuts its eyes and begins to gobble. All the hunter has to do is walk up and wring the gobbler's neck. "If a man had a ten-pound poke of gobble-weed," said Cummins, "he could ketch every dadblamed turkey in Taney County!"

Fox hunt: The unspeakable in pursuit of the uneatable.

— Oscar Wilde

* * * *

Many tall stories have grown up in Arkansas about the big flocks of pigeons, panthers, bears, wildcats, wolves, and smaller varmints that were always skulking around pigeon-roosts in order to pick up cripples. According to one tale, a hunter rode up beneath a roost near West Plains, Missouri, tied his horse to an overhanging limb, and went in pursuit of a wildcat. The shot that he fired at this animal frightened a great many pigeons away. Relieved of their weight, the tree sprang upright, jerking the hunter's horse high into the air. The poor beast hung there until the man could get an axe and cut the tree down!

"SORRY, DEAR, BUT FROM 150 METERS YOU LOOK LIKE A MOOSE!"

Doesn't know A from Izzard: A description of a stupid hunter who thinks he knows it all, but actually *doesn't know A from Izzard.*

* * * *

People on White River still remember the two Purdy brothers, who were always playing jokes on the summer visitors. A sportsman from Kansas City met them in the woods. The bigger boy carried a muzzle-loading shotgun, and the little one had a claw-hammer stuck in his belt. After some idle talk, the city feller asked why they carried the hammer. This was what the Purdy boys were waiting for. The younger one burst into tears. The tourist was profoundly shocked, but he persisted in questioning. Finally the boy told him that the Purdys lived mostly on squirrels. There was no money to buy shot, so they loaded the old gun with rusty nails. "Every squirrel we kill nowadays is nailed fast to the tree," sobbed the boy. "An' that big so-and-so," pointing to his brother, "makes me climb up an' pry 'em loose with this here claw-hammer!"

Don't holler till you're out of the woods: A way of saying, don't count your chickens before they're hatched.

* * * *

A half-legendary figure known in southwest Missouri as Abner Yancey is celebrated as the one-shot wonder of all time. Armed with a single-shot rifle, he was trying to get two squirrels lined up, so as to kill both of them with one bullet. The squirrels fell when Ab fired, and just then he "heerd turkeys a-yoikin'" in a nearby tree. Seven hens and a gobbler were sitting on a branch, and Ab's bullet had sped on to split the limb and catch their feet in the crack. Ab climbed the tree and wrung the turkeys' necks, but coming down he fell into a brush-pile, killing two big rabbits and a covey of quail. Wading into the creek, where one of the squirrels had fallen, he got his pockets and boot-tops full of fish! Ab reached back to scratch a chigger-bite, and one of the buttons popped off his shirt into a bunch of hazelbrush. A moment later he heard "a lot of gaspin' an' gurglin'" in the thicket and found a big buck rolling on the ground. Ab cut the animal's throat with his hunting-knife and found the lost button stuck in the deer's windpipe.

When Ab got home he had one deer, eight turkeys, two squirrels, two brush-rabbits, twenty-one quail and about fifty pounds of fish. "Pappy shore was proud when he seen me a-draggin' it all home," he said years later. "It was a sad day at our house, though, on account of Uncle Hen actin' up. Uncle Hen was a purty good feller, but he called me a liar when I was a-tellin' how I got that buck. Liar was allus a fightin' word in the Yancey family, so I just naturally had to kill him. I done it with my old huntin' knife, gentlemen, the same knife you-uns see a-stickin' out of my boot-top right now."

The old-timers tell me that the story of Ab Yancey's great hunt was believed by everybody in those days. "Anyhow," as one old fellow added with a grin, "I don't recollect hearin' it conterdicted none, so long as Ab was alive."

Some windy-spinners add the detail that after Ab's bullet split the limb and caught the turkeys it went on to penetrate a bee-tree, and Ab carried off a piggin of honey along with his other loot. A piggin is a homemade wooden bucket, and the story offers no explanation of how Ab got the piggin.

*   *   *   *

Give out: How a hunter feels after a long day hunting quail. He'd say, "I'm plumb *give out*."

*   *   *   *

Tall tales about bear hunting are legion in the Ozark country and are so ingeniously mingled with true stories and serious talk that it is sometimes hard to separate them. Right in the middle of an earnest discussion of big-game rifles, an old hunter in Fort Smith, Arkansas, told me that the main consideration in hunting bear is not to chase the animal too far before making the kill. "If you run a b'ar too much," said he, "it'll spile the meat every time. A fat old sow b'ar will run till she plumb cooks herself, if you don't watch out. I shot a b'ar once, down on the Ouachita, after she'd run about four mile. Yes, sir, an' the steam squirted out of the bullet-hole twenty foot high, a-spittin' an' a-hissin', an' misted up the whole valley like a July fog."

*   *   *   *

Not a tater in the patch: What you say when you haven't flushed a bird all day, and you are empty-handed, skunked, slim pickin's.

*   *   *   *

A certain fleet-footed Arkansawyer, according to the fireside legends, always shot his bear in such a way as to injure, but not seriously cripple it. Then he would run for home, with the enraged animal in close pursuit. When he reached the cabin, he would turn and shoot the bear dead. He figured it was easier than skinning and cutting up the critter out in the woods somewhere, and then packing the meat and skin home, on his back. This way, the old woman and the kids could do most of the work.

"I finally bagged him, but I had to chase him thirty miles to do it."

American Legion Magazine. December 1957

Slew or slue: One heckuva lot of game, as, "We killed a *slue* of them birds."

* * * *

Fred Starr tells of an Ozark boy who was knocking squirrels out of the tall trees with rocks, always throwing with his left hand. A pop-eyed city feller remarked about the astounding accuracy of southpaws. "I ain't left-hand-ed," the boy said, "but if I was to throw right-handed, it'd tear the squirrels up too bad."

He couldn't hit the ground with his hat: A description of a lousy shot, as, "That sucker didn't kill a single bird, and they was flushin' all around us. Why, *he couldn't hit the ground with his hat.*"

＊　＊　＊　＊

Down around Eureka Springs, Arkansas, the boys make use of an ingenious trick to catch rabbits, according to a gentleman in the Basin Park Hotel. The boys paint round black spots, about six inches in diameter, upon the ends of saw-logs lying upon the ground. Then they send their dogs into the brush to stir up the rabbits. When a rabbit sees one of these round black spots on the end of a log he thinks it's a hole, and when he tries to run into it he knocks himself unconscious. All the boys have to do is pick 'em up and put 'em in a sack.

＊　＊　＊　＊

Ain't worth the shot it'd take to send him to hell: as, "You call that new guide a good man? Why, that bugger *ain't worth the shot it'd take to send him to hell.*"

＊　＊　＊　＊

Near Cyclone, Missouri, I heard an oft-repeated yarn about a man attacked by a bear in broad daylight, right in the public road. He was unarmed, but snatched up a good throwin' rock and cast it with great force into the bear's open mouth, and thence down the creature's throat. The bear swung round and fled, but the hillman was fully aroused now, so he grabbed another flint-rock and dashed in pursuit. When he threw the second stone it entered the animal's rectum with such force that it met the first missile somewhere in the middle of the bear's body. As the two flints struck together, they produced sparks. The bear was fat, and its body took fire instantly and burned up like a barrel of oil. Nothing was left but a wide circle of scorched earth and a pile of blackened bones. "That'll learn bears not to monkey with me," said the hillman.

On the go down: Diminishing energy, health, interest, as, "I cain't go huntin' 'cause my rheumatiz is *on the go down.*"

* * * *

The business of the turkeys carrying a man through the air is not uncommon in tales of this kind. "When I was a little chap," said old man Linkletter of Little Rock, Arkansas, "I was a great hand to sneak up on birds an' rabbits, an' ketch 'em with my hands. One time I seen some wild turkeys eatin' corn out of the chinks of our corncrib. I snuck up easy-like, an' grabbed two big gobblers by their legs. But they was too big for me, an' the next thing I knowed we was way up in the air, lookin' down on the trees. I was a great hand to figger things out in them days. I knowed that if I turned loose I'd be killed sure, an' every second I held on they was takin' me higher up an' further off from home. But then I figgered if I was to let one of 'em loose, the other'n might take me down safe. So I turned the biggest one loose. The other gobbler he flopped his best, but I was a little too heavy for him. So down we come, easy like one of these here parachutes. I was aimin' to wring his neck when we got down, but he flopped his wings an' drug me around in the briars till I finally give up an' turned him loose. I had to walk six miles to git home, an' Paw give me a lickin'. But I reckon I was pretty lucky, at that. If I hadn't figgered out what to do, I might have got hurt some way."

* * * *

Sign: Manure or droppings of wildlife, a "sign" that they've passed this way.

* * * *

Bear Sign: The signature (sign) of a bear. In cowboy palaver, it is "a doughnut."

Old man Taylor was bragging about his tree-dog. "Just last night" said he, "that there pup kilt the biggest coon I ever seen. God-a-mighty boys, that coon was four foot long, an' must of weighed a hundred pound! He'll meat the whole family a month, an' we're a-goin' to use his hide for a wagon-cover!" A few days later the game warden arrested Taylor for killing fur-bearing animals out of season. "They fined me ten dollars, boys," the old man complained loudly. "Ten dollars, just for havin' one measly little coonskin, not much bigger'n a chipmunk!"

"NEXT TIME MAKE SURE HE'S DEAD."

Tight enough to crack a tick on: How your belly feels after you've eaten too much.

"It happened about six years ago when a truthful friend was hunting deer on a mountain in British Columbia. He had covered quite a bit of rugged terrain when he spotted a beautiful buck in some underbrush on a ridge a little way off. With a well placed shot, he dropped the buck in its tracks and, with some excitement, hurried to the fallen animal. His excitement soon dwindled, however, when the realization dawned that it would take some doing to get the buck back to his truck at the foot of the mountain.

"It was while he was considering possibilities of how he was going to accomplish this problem single-handed that he was startled by a noise behind and turned to see the game warden approaching.

"After the game warden had stopped by my friend and puffed and wheezed for a minute, catching his breath, he remarked as how he had heard the shot and come to investigate. He then asked to see my friend's hunting license, which, my friend told him, he didn't have on him.

"On hearing this, the game warden informed my friend that he was taking him in and was taking the deer along as evidence.

"When they reached the bottom of the mountain where the game warden's car and my friend's truck were parked, my friend happened to put his hand into his pocket and pulled out his wallet, exclaiming, "Well, what do you know! I had my hunting license with me all the time!"

— Roger Lindsay. ARGOSY MAGAZINE.
Reprinted by permission of Argosy Communications, Inc.
Copyright © 1990 Argosy Communications, Inc.
All Rights Reserved.

✳   ✳   ✳   ✳

A plump pigeon at a shootin' match: Used when you want to warn someone inexperienced and defenseless to stay away, as, "You're about as fit to take care of yourself in the woods as *a plump pigeon at a shootin' match.*"

The following four stories are from a game warden's books! Yesiree bob! It's true! Title? *GAME WARDEN? SHOOT THE S.O.B.* Harold Hoey, 1425 E. Eastwood, Marshall, MO. 65340.

There was a "Would Be" dog trainer who had managed to train and sell a couple or three dogs, but he had one dog that just wasn't showing too well. So he decided that in order to move it, he would need a gimmick. This little bitch was a sharp and affectionate dog, but she was lacking something when it came to quail and performing in the field. He decided to concentrate on her intelligence and affectionate qualities. A couple of days later, a guy called to see if he had a good dog for sale. The trainer assured him that he did have a very sharp dog that was ready to go, so they planned to meet at the kennel early the next day for a trial run. The trainer let the dog out of the pen and gave the command "Sit," and the dog obeyed without hesitation. He then said, "Shake hands with the nice man," and the dog did as she was told. He then ordered the dog to get into the trunk and sit. The hunter was definitely impressed. They drove down to the field and the trainer instructed the dog to hunt up the birds. The dog took off, coursing the field well, when all of a sudden she jumped about four feet right straight up in the air. The startled hunter said, "What the hell kind of maneuver was that?" and the trainer replied, "I told you that dog was real smart — there was a fence there last year."

* * * *

From kin see to cain't see: To hunt from dawn to dark.

* * * *

A couple of city hunters were driving the back roads looking for a place to hunt when they came across an old run-down place, and one of the hunters thought he knew this farmer and had hunted there before.

He went in the house and was recognized by the farmer. They visited a few minutes and the farmer asked him to do a favor. "See that old swayback horse out there? He is over 30 years old and can just barely get around. Acts like he is suffering, too, and I wonder if you would put him out of his misery for me."

The hunter said, "I don't really look forward to it, but I will do it for you."

On the way back to the car, the hunter (a practical joker) decided to play a little joke on his buddy. He jerked open the back door, grabbed his deer rifle from the back seat and grumbled. "The old bastard said we couldn't hunt on his place and to get the hell out of here. I'll show the old grouch," and with that comment he shot the old horse right between the eyes.

About that time he heard two more shots and he turned to see that his buddy had shot two of the farmer's cows. The story goes that this guy gave up practical jokes after they finished paying for the cows.

* * * *

Slaunchwise: Diagonal, slanting, as, "That deer cut across the field *slaunchwise*...and I missed him."

* * * *

A couple of old quail hunting buddies met at their Ozark cabin for their usual opening-weekend hunt. Everything was perfect — they got up a number of nice coveys, the old dog worked like every quail hunter dreams a dog would. They didn't miss too many good shots and limited out early in the evening.

When they got back to the cabin, they built a nice fire in the fireplace and enjoyed a nice supper that they had prepared in advance that was waiting for them in the oven. They were relaxing and having an after dinner drink with the old setter, Mac, on the throw rug in front of them. Old Mac sat up, yawned, and proceeded to start licking his privates, as male dogs are prone to do.

The first hunter turned to his buddy and in an attempt to be funny said, "I wish to hell I could do that."

The second hunter answered, "Well, I guess you can if you want to that badly, but I would advise you to pet him a little first."

* * * *

Give out: To state or acknowledge a fact, as, "That Pete Jones done *give out* that he's got him the best coon dog in these parts."

" SEE, BOY? I ALWAYS TOLD YOU THAT YOU WERE A GOOD HUNTING DOG. "

Rode hard and put up wet: Describes a field trialer's long day, riding in rain and coming home soaked to the skin. This is cowboy language but fits all outdoors.

* * * *

Old Shorty showed up with his truckload of dogs a little late. He was hurriedly unloading them when he noticed that his favorite, a little speckled bitch, was coming in heat. He figured she could mess up the race, so he put her in the cab of the truck and took off through the woods with the rest of the pack to get them in the race. Well, that little bitch wasn't used to being left behind and put up quite a commotion. A little boy, who had stayed behind with the trucks, heard and saw the fit this dog was having and decided that she needed to be in the race, and he opened the door. Old Shorty recognized Speck's bawl mouth and knew somehow she had gotten out. He took out in hot pursuit, but before long, the dogs had gotten clear out of hearing.

Shorty went back to the truck and started down the road in the direction he had last heard them. He had gone several miles when he met a farmer driving a cow down the road and he rolled down the window and asked the farmer if he had seen a pack of hounds chasing a fox with a little speckled bitch trailing behind. The farmer said, "Nope, I didn't see that, but I did see a pack of hounds come by here a bit ago, the little speckled bitch was in the lead and the fox was running fourth."

✳ ✳ ✳ ✳

A fellow was telling me about an ad he saw in the paper under PETS, LOST OR STRAYED. The ad was as follows: Strayed, English Setter. Has mangled left ear, blind in right eye, has broken tail and carries his left hind leg, recently castrated. Answers to the name, "Lucky".

✳ ✳ ✳ ✳

Arguing with him is like a rabbit kickin' against a mule! Useless!

✳ ✳ ✳ ✳

Winchester quarantine: The phrase has the affect of a KEEP OUT sign, or a sign that reads, NO HUNTING ALLOWED. It simplifies and reinforces an order to get the hell out and stay out of certain grounds, grounds under *Winchester quarantine*.

"HE WAS A GOOD OL' HUNTIN' DOG...
SURE DID LOVE HIS CIGARS, THOUGH."

A man met a panther on a narrow ledge to which he had fled when pursued by a she-bear with cubs. He couldn't go forward because of the panther. He couldn't turn back because of the bear. Resolutely he drew his knife, but the panther knocked it out of his hand. The great cat opened wide its mouth when the intrepid hunter had a sudden inspiration. Springing forward, he reached down the varmint's throat, caught hold of the root of its tail, and with one swift pull he turned the critter inside out! Leaping over the body of the ruined panther, he left it lying there to distract the attention of the bear, which was still following close on his trail.

* * * *

Bottom rail gittin' on top: Describes a beginning hunter who is rapidly getting better.

Gone Goose: Dead or disappeared as, "That blamed pointer of mine took off three days ago and ain't got back yet. I figure he's a *gone goose.*

* * * *

Goose drownder: A heavy rain, a flooding storm.

* * * *

There's a wacky character called Happy Pete who shot the bill off a woodpecker so neatly that the bird went on pecking for a full minute before he discovered his loss.

* * * *

Haven't seen you in a coon's age: An old phrase meaning in a long time, *a coon's age.*

* * * *

It was only a few miles from Bentonville, according to one ancient tale, that George Spellman raised a mongrel foxhound named Booger. George declared that Booger was a perfect blend of many famous strains — Walker, Trigg, July, Birdsong, Bluetick, Goodman, Redbone, and Trumbo. The local foxhunters laughed at these claims, but did not deny Booger's value as a general purpose potlicker.

When George carried his big Winchester, Booger chased deer and ignored all other game. If the weapon was a squirrel rifle, the dog treed squirrels exclusively. When George brought out a shotgun, Booger would point quail like a bird dog. If he started out at night with a lantern, old Booger rushed on ahead to trail coons and possums as well as any tree dog in Arkansas. One day, so the story goes, George appeared at the gate with a cane fishpole over his shoulder. Booger hesitated only a moment, then snatched up a tin bucket and started a-digging for worms.

Some dogs act like hired hands and others act like true executives. Here are a couple of Ozark stories to illustrate the two types. The first story illustrates the kind of individual who might be a building and loan executive. The second story seems of a type more like a banker.

Sam Garroute, who lives not far from Aurora, Missouri, always claimed to have the best tree dog in the country. Smartest dog that ever lived, said Sam. Always knew just what sort of varmints were to be pursued. Ozark hunters "case" all skins nowadays, stretching them on boards made for the purpose. A skunk requires a board of a particular size and shape; a coon another; a mink still another. When Sam wanted to hunt coons, he just set a coon-board outside the door; if he wanted possums, he set out a possum-board, and so forth. The dog always located the proper varmint and ignored all other species. One day Sam's wife was redding up the house, and happened to set her ironing board outside for a few moments, just to get it out of the way. The dog gazed at it openmouthed; there is no wild animal in the Ozarks whose skin could cover such a big stretchin'-board as that. The brag dog howled dismally and slunk off into the woods. That was seven years ago, and the dog has never been seen since. "I reckon he's still a-huntin'," Sam told the boys in a barbershop at Aurora.

✳   ✳   ✳   ✳

The preceding story told of a faithful, if dumb dog, one that hunted without imagination. But there are all kinds of dogs, just as there are all kinds of people. Just take a look at this smart, reasonable dog. Why, this dog would make an executive vice president in most any American corporation. See if you don't agree.

Tommy, he had this dog. Tommy, he's a kinda lazy fellow, you know. He didn't like to do anything unless he had to. Got up late and sat around all evening. That kind of thing. So, it was aggravating for him to go out coon-huntin' and come back in and find he didn't have a skin board the right size to put the skin on. If he got him a big coon, he'd only have him a small skin board, and he'd have to stop to make a new big skin board. If he got him a little coon, why the skin board would be too big and small skin wouldn't fit it. They's always a problem.

Now Tommy was smart even if he was lazy, and his dogs were noted for being uncommon smart. He trained them in all sorts of tricks, and jobs, too! Oh, they would roll over, and count, and even multiply. Well, he trained one of the dogs to tree coons the right size for his skin boards. He'd hold up a skin board for the dog before he ever went out.

The dog would then go and get him a coon to fit the skin board.

Well, that worked fine, except that the dog, it disappeared. And, of course, Tommy worried about him because he'd always been a faithful dog. He finally figured out what happened to him. You know, his wife Carolyn had put the ironing board out on the back porch, and Tommy figured that dog was probably out there still lookin' for a coon big enough to fit it.

Now, folks down there around Brasstown, North Carolina, they scoff at that. They just didn't believe that could be the truth. They said that somebody just swiped that dog or he got killed or lost or something like that, you know. But I was telling Bill Sparks about that — he lives out there near Paint Lick, here in Kentucky, runs the slaughterhouse — any of you know him? Plays the banjo and everything, a good fella. I was telling him about Tommy's dog.

"Well, no," he says, "that dog's not lost. It was out looking for a big coon, and it heard there were some big ones up here in Kentucky. So it came up here around Paint Lick, and it's got it a big coon. It's got the coon penned up not far from here cause he's not quite big enough yet and he's feeding him on corn to try to make it grow a little more. Then he'll take him back to North Carolina.

— Dr. John Ramsay — Berea, KY

Git in the go 'long: To get started at hunting or fishing. To "get moving," as, "We best *git in the go 'long* or we ain't never gonna git us no birds."

＊ ＊ ＊ ＊

Here's one that was told on Liars' Night at a fox-hunters' convention near Guthrie, Oklahoma. There was a field contest between a valuable pedigreed coon hound owned by a Tulsa sportsman and a mongrel belonging to a local boy. The pedigreed dog passed a certain big oak without a sound, but the mongrel stopped and barked "treed." The hunters saw no trace of a coon, and couldn't even find any hole in the tree. But the mongrel refused to leave, so the judges finally ordered the tree cut down, to satisfy the dog's owner.

The trunk was split open, and showed a small cavity that had grown over twenty-five years ago, according to a count of the annual rings. In the hollow was the skeleton of a coon, dead for at least a quarter of a century! "A coon hound," said the owner of the mongrel, "has got to foller a cold trail or else he ain't no good. That there dog of mine," he added, "is a real coon-ketcher."

＊ ＊ ＊ ＊

Bossloper: A woods hunter or trapper.

＊ ＊ ＊ ＊

"One time I was out a-huntin', and I come around a swag into a kind of little open space under a big shagbark hickory, and I seen this squirrel. I raised my gun to shoot it, and then I took thought and said to myself, 'Why, no; I can't kill that squirrel. He's too old. I'll just let the old feller alone. He's the oldest squirrel I ever seen. He must a been a hunnerd years old.'"

"How'd you know he was so old?"

"He was a-settin' there crackin' hickory nuts with a rock!"

Laughter In Appalachia. Loyal Jones and Billy Edd Wheeler.
1987. August House Little Rock, AR.

"NOW *THAT'S* A GUN DOG"

He stuck to that feller like a squirrel to a knot: A determined fighter, or, a loyal friend.

✳ ✳ ✳ ✳

Now comes a story similar to one told by Abraham Lincoln. For all we know, it could very well have its origin with Methusaleh. And yet it is still one of the best ever told.

Sometimes the ability of these pioneer dogs not only to hold but to detect quarry was absolutely uncanny:

"There was once a guy who had a dog he was very proud of. He would hold a point on any bird for any length of time. He was in a bar with the dog and the dog suddenly jumped up and went into a point at another guy who had just walked into the bar. The dog's owner could not see anything that might have caused the dog's behavior. He asked the man, 'Do you happen to have a bird in your pocket?'

"'No," he answered.

"Well, I am certainly sorry my dog is behaving like this," the dog's owner apologized. "I hope that it hasn't embarrassed you too much, Mr...? Mr...?"

"Partridge," the man answered.

"WHAT A HUNTING TRIP, MOM — DAD GOT A COW AND A PICKUP TRUCK!"

Duck: Not all "ducks" fly and make good eating. There is a "duck" used in hospitals...as a urinal, and it is duck-shaped. In such hospitals it could be said that, "They put you to bed with a *duck*."

Pea Turkey: Nothing at all as, e.g., when the game warden asks, "Didn't they tell you there was no hunting on this farm? Didn't you see that NO HUNTING sign?"

"Nope. They didn't say *pea turkey* about it."

✳ ✳ ✳ ✳

Back in the 1870s, out in Nebraska, they told some real doozies! Just take a look at this one:

There was a standing bet at the saloon of this little western town that the man did not live who could swear, truly swear that he had seen 100,000 buffalo at one time. If proven, the man could have free drinks for a week.

Several men said they had seen that many, and more buffalo, but they refused to swear to it. At last a man named Eldridge came to town, and he was willing to swear he'd seen 100,000 buffalo at one time.

"Tell us about it. But first, you must take an oath as to the truth of what you are about to tell us. Hold up your right hand. Do you swear to tell the truth, the whole truth and nothing but the truth?"

"I do."

"You may continue," the bartender directed.

"Well, sir," Eldridge began, "I was a boy coming west in a wagon train. We had made it just a smidgen north of the Platte when a huge herd of buffalo came up on us. We had to corral all our wagons and stock to keep from gettin' overrun by the buffalo. But our men sure had good huntin'. Those fellers shot buffalo for a week! They shot so fast, and their guns heated the air so hot we could hardly stand stayin' in our clothes. On the eighth day the herd kinda spread out and gave us time to get across that river Platte. And I tell you this...it was a damn good thing we got across when we did..."

"Why?" someone yelled.

"Why! Hell, man, we'd no more than got across when we looked back and there come the main herd!"

Two fellows were hunting out in west Texas. Night came on and they cooked supper and then spread blankets. But first they strung a rawhide rope in a circle around them just to keep the rattlesnakes away. Everyone knows snakes won't cross a rawhide rope. One guy awakened only to see that two snakes were holding up the rope while two more were crawling underneath! It was told that both men hit El Paso in one jump.

* * * *

Right many: A lot, more than a few, as, "He hunted all day and come home with a *right many* rabbits."

* * * *

There was a great hunter from Wheeling,
Filled full with such delicate feeling,
When he read, on the door,
"Don't spit on the floor,"
He up and did spat on the ceiling.

* * * *

Poor as snakes: In bad condition, thin, as "The deer out there were *poor as snakes*, this year."

* * * *

Jeb, my Air Force buddy from Texas, had bored me half to death with his Texas tales. So you can imagine how delighted I was when we both got transferred to Alaska, our "biggest" state in the Union. But this didn't stop Jeb. All our free time was spent in the nearby town's general store where Jeb told endless tales about the wonders of Texas and Texans.

After a few weeks of this, the boys were quite fed up, and one trapper remarked that he didn't think Jeb could pass the test of becoming an Alaskan.

"Test? What test?" asked Jeb.

"'Well," said the grizzled old trapper, "to become an Alaskan you have to do three things. First, you have to drink a quart of sourdough whiskey. Second, you have to track down a Kodiak bear. Third, you have to make love to an Eskimo woman. If you do all this, you can qualify as an honorary Alaskan."

"Hearing this, Jeb promptly grabbed the jug of hootch from the old-timer, toasted Texas and drained the jug without lowering it from his lips till it was dry. Then, somewhat red-faced and wild-eyed, he staggered out the door and wasn't seen again until almost four hours later when he returned, battered and bruised in his now tattered uniform.

"'What happened to you?' was the astonished trapper's query.

"Shucks, ah jest met your second test, pahdner. Now who's this here Eskimo woman ah'm supposed to track down?"

— George R. Somick — ARGOSY MAGAZINE
Reprinted by permission of Argosy Communications, Inc.
Copyright © 1990. Argosy Communications, Inc.
All rights reserved.

* * * *

Barrel of shucks: Worthless, as, "That guide we hired to hunt deer wasn't worth a *barrel of shucks.*"

* * * *

The BURLINGTON LIARS CLUB of Burlington, Wisconsin, has been a major factor in keeping that most American form of humor, the tall tale, alive, thriving and most entertaining in the United States of America. And the club still thrives, collects tall tales, publishes them and continues to keep this unique aspect of American culture going strong. Here are three of their great stories.

* * * *

For a lot of years I have been working to perfect a duck call. Satisfied with my laboratory tests, I recently decided to give it a field trial. The first time I blew the call, ducks swarmed in from all directions; the sky was black with them. I cut loose with my pump gun and with six shots killed my limit of six ducks. What is so strange about that you say? Well, when I picked up those ducks I found that three of them were decoys!

"IT'S A FAWN..."

I hunt regularly with an old mule trained to run jack rabbits down. I was hunting one day and chased a jack rabbit for miles. Finally the rabbit ran over a 1,000 foot cliff. The mule and I dived after him. I was worried for a minute as we fell through space. But when we were within ten feet of the bottom I recovered my wits.

"Whoa, there," I shouted. And that mule was so darned well trained he stopped dead in his tracks right in the air. I got off and gently dropped the remaining few feet.

— Verne L. Osborn — Burlington Liars Club

* * * *

The rabbits down this way are so fast that we use high powered rifles to hunt them instead of shotguns. Even then, hunters never get any unless they know the tricks. To bag these rabbits on the run you have to aim, shoot fast and then let out a shrill whistle. When you

whistle, the rabbit stops and the bullet has a chance to
catch up with him.

—— Shelton R. Day —— Burlington Liars Club

* * * *

Siftin' dust: Same as "light a shuck." What you do when
you see the game warden coming and you don't have
your license, as, "When that game warden started
towards us, why man I just naturally took to *siftin' dust*."

* * * *

One of the founders and a past president of The
Burlington Liars' Club was O.C. Hulett who in 1935, published a superb tall-tale collection: NOW I'LL TELL ONE.
This hilarious collection was set in mythical Coon Hollow
where, on the porch of Zeb Whittaker's store, the town
met to exchange windies, whoppers, blanket-stretchers
or, if you prefer, tall tales.

Here are two tales from NOW I'LL TELL ONE.

"But good shootin' isn't everythin'. Get yourself
corralled by a bunch of hostiles that outnumber you five
to one and all your fast shootin' in the world ain't goin' to
do you a heap of good — they'll down you in the end.
You got to use your head. Jest to show you — ever one
of you shoot a hell-diver?"

Negative answers and shakes of the head
answered his query as he looked around the circle.

"Thought so. They're jest too fast to be shot. I
found that out up on the headwaters of the Arkansas. I
seen one of those pesky fowl out there in an eddy and
wantin' to try out my shootin' hand, I let drive at him.
Well, he jest ducked under and came up again big as life.
I must have shot a dozen times, and never touched a
feather.

"Made me mad, it did, to get took in by a fool bird,
so I set me down and got out my pipe to smoke on it. All
the while this fool diver kept on watchin' me. First I
knowed he was divin' again. Then I figured it out. Every
time I give a puff of smoke from my pipe, he dived jest

like he did when he saw the puff of smoke come out of the end of my rifle.

"Well," concluded Grandpa, getting up and sauntering across the porch to the top of the steps, "it happened then like it always does when anythin' — bird or man — that thinks it's smart goes up against someone smarter. I couldn't kill that fool bird by shootin' — but I smoked six pipes of tobacco and drowned him! So long, boys." And Grandpa Skinner, cocking his hat over his right eye, strolled down the steps and off in the direction of his home.

＊　＊　＊　＊

"I had a blue-tick hound one time 'fore I moved to town; Skinny will recall him, he hunted back of him many a time. And he was the smartest, fastest houn' dog that ever run a rabbit on Wildcat Ridge.

"Show you how smart he was. He tagged along one morning when I went out to chop wood. I didn't pay much attention to him, 'cause it was downright cold that day. Matter of fact, it was so cold and frosty the old axe just echoed when I drove it into a tree. I got my load of wood cut, and started home, and darned if I didn't find another load laying alongside the track that the echo of my axe had cut — but that ain't what I started out to tell you.

"Here I am chopping away for dear life, and all of a sudden I hear a hound baying over in the tamarack. Pretty soon a rabbit comes past me lickety-split, and I think, 'Well, old Trailer is putting them up,' but there ain't nothing I can do about it, and I keep on chopping. Pretty soon another one goes by, and I take a look to see where he goes and darned if there ain't old Trailer sitting on a stump, big as life. You see, that darned dog was a ventriloquist, and he was just throwing his voice over there into the swamp."

"I expect his voice got lost over there in the tamarack and you had to kill him because he couldn't bay the trail no more?" suggested Doc Rock.

"Oh, no, Doc, nothing like that," replied Big Jeb easily, "it was his speed that killed him in the end. That fall I was hunting rabbits with him and he got one up in the headland on one end of the cornfield. The darned cottontail lit out down the corn row, with old Trailer gaining on him every jump. You know how shifty a rabbit is. Well, at the end of that row the rabbit whirled to one side, went up about six rows and started back. I took a shot at him and knocked him kicking, but old Trailer didn't come over to pick him up. I thought that was funny and when I went down to look, darned if he wasn't laying dead at the end of the row.

"When the rabbit sidestepped, old Trailer was going full speed. Matter of fact, he was going so fast that when he tried to stop, his backbone ran right up through his brain and killed him in his tracks."

* * * *

"It's a fact," the enthusiastic hunter said, "that hunting is not forbidden! Because if God hadn't meant for mankind to hunt he'd not have given us wool socks and plaid shirts."

* * * *

Poke: A game bag. You could say, "Put them quail in your *poke* and let's go home."

* * * *

Grandpa began his story, "I mind the time I trapped the winter with Crazy Jim up in a hole in those high mountains on the north fork of the Platte up where she heads. Beaver was thick and Injuns scarce, so after a while, long toward spring, we got kind of keerless and left our guns at the cabin when we went to make the rounds of the trap line. And bein' keerless like that like to caused the end of Crazy Jim."

"Did the Indians catch him, Grandpa?" asked Skinny.

"No, Skinny," replied that worthy, "it wasn't Injuns; it was wolves. A pack of 'em got onto Jim's trail one mornin' and almost nabbed him afore he could shinny up a big cottonwood tree. Once up the tree Jim figured he was safe, 'cause it was two foot through and fifty foot to the first limbs. Jim figured all he had to do was outsit the wolves, and after half an hour or so it looked like he was right, 'cause a half dozen of 'em went slinkin' off into the brush. But the rest jest set down on their tails and waited, and by Godfrey, it wasn't half an hour afore those wolves that had left, came pikin' back herdin' six beaver ahead of 'em and danged if they didn't set them beaver to work cuttin' down that tree!

"Now, an ordinary man would have been stumped, but old Jim he did some fast figuring. He crawled out on one of the long limbs, and sure enough, those wolves follered him, wantin' to be underneath when he dropped. So, Jim got right busy, and he wove the limbs of that cottonwood tree into a regular cage on all sides except the one that it was goin' to fall on, and then he pulled off the limbs.

"When she started to fall, all those wolves rushed over to get the first bite out of old Jim, but he squirreled around onto the top side of that cage he had wove, and darned if he didn't trap a whole bunch of 'em."

"And I suppose he came home with twenty-five wolf skins to boot," hazarded Skinny.

"Wolf skins, wolf skins," Grandpa snapped at him. "Shows how much you know about things. Nobody bothered with wolf skins those days, they wasn't worth packin' home. But he never overlooked a chance, old Jim didn't. He ketched and skun those six beaver afore they could get back into the river!"

"I'll bet your pardner carried his rifle after that experience," suggested Big Jed.

"Not he," returned Grandpa, glancing over the porch rail to see how far the shadow had progressed. "He was all set up over how he had out-cuted those wolves, and besides the darned thing was heavy to lug around. Why, that gun that Crazy Jim used was so big that he used a tame pack-rat to clean it. Jim used to pour bear grease in through the nipple, where you set the cap.

Then he would put the rat in the muzzle and he'd crawl down the barrel to get the grease. When Jim could hear him gnawing away at the grease, he used to haul him out with a rawhide string he tied to his tail."

"Could he shoot very straight with a gun as big as that?" Eben Doolittle wanted to know.

"Shoot straight? Say, if you told him to hit an Injun in the eye at a half a mile, Jim would ask you which eye you wanted," Grandpa retorted.

"That's pretty straight shooting," remarked Slivers Kees, "but those old muzzle loaders couldn't shoot very fast. Now I remember hearing Grandad Kees tell about a fellow they called Wild Bill Hickok. He was the fastest pistol shot of them all, by Grandad's tell. Grandad saw him perform out at Hays City, Kansas, one time when they was building the Union Pacific railroad.

"This Wild Bill stuck a good big darning needle into a post about four rods back from the track. Then they put him on a flat car and backed the train a few miles up the track. Starting back, Bill waited till the train got to rolling about sixty miles an hour. Then he picked up his rifle and fired a shot in the general direction of that needle. Dropping his rifle and whipping out his six shooters, he began shooting at that rifle bullet. By hitting it first one side and then the other, he herded it right up in line with the eye of that needle. The pistol bullets had been clipping off pieces right along and by this time he had that rifle bullet whittled down to about the right size, so with his last shot, he hit it square, and drove it right through the eye of that needle!"

* * * *

Arkansas is known for its ability to build tall, very tall stories, truly whackin' good tales. And Vance Randolph was the master who collected the very best of them. Here are a couple of blanket-stretchers (tall tales, to the uninitiated).

A politician near Mena, Arkansas, was mighty proud of his new shotgun. It was a ten-bore, which is two sizes larger than most of the guns used in the Ozarks nowadays. One day he was bragging about the piece in a tavern west of Mauldin, when a villager brought out an eight-gauge goose gun, a really gigantic thing. The politician had never seen such a gun before; it made his own pride and joy look like a child's pea-shooter. After awhile an old hunter remarked that he had a much larger shotgun at home.

"Bigger'n that eight-bore?" cried the office-seeker. "For God's sake, how big is it?"

The old man hesitated. "Well, I cain't exactly call the number of it," he said, "but it's a pretty big gun. Whenever it needs cleanin', we just grease a groundhog an' run him through the barr'l."

Long ago I heard the story of some country boys in Lonoke County, Arkansas, who built a very large muzzle-loading shotgun, the barrel was made of water-pipe taken from an abandoned hotel. The thing was mounted on a wagon, to be fired at wild geese feeding in the fields. At the first discharge the gun busted and tore the wagon all to hell, but didn't hurt the hunters, since the trigger was pulled by means of a long cord. The explosion killed seventy-five geese and crippled many more. Most of the geese were not struck by shot, but by fragments of the water-pipe barrel.

"It made a noise like thunder, only louder," I was told. "The cows for miles around gave sour milk for the rest of the week!"

*   *   *   *

There's a hunting lodge in northern Michigan where the bulletin board lists the game killed that season, along with the names of the members who got the game. Opposite the name of one worthy member is this stunning record of his greatest accomplishment: "George Elliot: A record! Eight cases of Canadian Club!"

*   *   *   *

There's a famous fable, perhaps told by Aesop, concerning a skunk, a lion and a hawk who were debating as to which one was the most dangerous and feared animal in the jungle.

The hawk claimed top dog: "I win because I hit 'em from above and, from above, I got the best view of all. I see things nobody else does!"

The lion rejoined: "Nonsense! I'm the most powerful animal of all, with the longest, sharpest teeth and claws. I'm the most dangerous, for sure!"

Then the skunk said: "I have the power to stink up the whole jungle and run out every man or beast in the territory."

And so they argued, on and on, until a big old bear came ambling along and swallowed the three of 'em — Hawk, Lion and Stinker!

First hunter: "You ever been deer huntin', Ed?"

Second hunter: "Dang right. I shot a buck, once."

First hunter: "You did? Tell me about it."

Second hunter: "Well, I fired away and shot a buck. Then I shot another..."

First hunter: "Wow! You were some lucky. Then what'd you do?"

Second hunter: "Somebody hollared, 'Here come the cops!' so I dropped the dice and got out of there."

* * * *

Bullet: A real wowser, a winner, a son of a gun, as, "Thet ol' boy is s-o-o-me *bullet*."

* * * *

Everybody knows that during a campaign for state office, most candidates will weasel around questions in trying to please all sides and offend none. One of the best examples occurred when a certain state senator ran for re-election and was asked to give his views on a certain piece of hunting legislation that regulated just where and how many deer could be taken.

A man in the audience stood up and was recognized. "Senator, our deer huntin' club is gathered here to find out just how you stand on this law that is going to regulate how we hunt. Are you for it or not?"

"I'm pleased that you asked me, sir. I aim to let my public know exactly how I stand on that question. I've studied hard to arrive at an answer. You see, I canvassed the district and I find that half of my friends are for it and half of them are against it. Now, my friends, I swear to you here and now, that I am not now, or ever, going to let my friends down. I stand by 'em always!"

* * * *

What did the lion say when he saw two hunters in a jeep? "Meals on wheels."

Until recent generations, the folk of Tennessee often used a poetic biblical language not generally heard in this country. Whether they used it well or not is another question. So proceed to read this oft-told tale with a biblical aura about it....as well as the more earthy aura of the Tennessee mountains.

THE GREAT TENNESSEE FOX HUNT

Now hit come to pass in the reign of Henry Horton, Governor of Tennessee, thot Ex-Governor Alf Taylor waxed ole an' well stricken in years an' the Nimrods of his native County of Carter said one to another:

"Go to. Let us even have a great Fox Hunt in honor of our distinguished fellow citizen, ere he departs unto the Happy Huntin' Groun', fer verily he hath been our leader in the Chase as well as politics."

So great preparation wuz made. They slew the fatted calf an' two sheep an' three swine an' digged a great trench over which to roast them whar-with-all. An' they did go unto Churches an' hotels an' the Country Club an' borrowed vessels of china an' knives an' forks of silver. An' they pitched a tent an' set a day fer the feast. An' they sont forth messengers bearin' invitations unto the great of the land. Moreover, they did buy a fox an put hit in a cage.

Also they did provide 100 measures — measured well and truly in half-gallon fruit jars — of strong drink made from the corn of East Tennessee, an' they sont word unto the Philistines, thot air to say, the Sheriff an' his Deputies, thot they were not invited.

Now on the 13th day of the fourth month of the one thousandth nineteen hundredth and twentyeight year, on the day of the feast, the people gathered themselves together from Dan unto Beersheba, even a great multitude of 5000 men, so thot they overflowed the tent an' covered the whole of Bogard's Knob.

An' they did eat an' drink, yea, they an' their houn' dogs with them.

Now hit come to pass thot as evenin' come on, Gov. Horton made a great speech an' Uncle Alf did play on his fiddle an' they made merry until some Son of Beliel, who wot not what he done by reason of the strong drink, did hurl one of the vessels of china into the midst of the gathering. Wharupon all them present tuck up vessels of china an' hurled them each at his neighbor, so thot the hotel and church property were utterly destroyed. Moreover, they tuck away the knives an' forks of silver fer a remembrance.

Now darkness come on an' the houn's did yell loudly thot the fox mout be released, but the present company did completely fergit the business in hand, an' forming groups about the fruit jars, beguiled the hours of night with song an' story.

Thus hit come to pass thot no man knoweth what become of the fox. But hit air thought thot someone fell over his cage an' thot he walked outten the open door an' gat himself unto the hills an' escaped.

Now those present had come in rubber tired chariots, thot could in nowise steer theyselves, so thot great confusion prevailed, fer the host did become so intangled thot they had to wait fer break of day to disengage an' depart unto they homes.

Thus did end an' come to naught the celebrated fox chase wharin the fox were not chased.

After them days the tribe of the Fox Hunters Association hid themselves out in dens and caves of the mountains, fer the hotels and churches breathed dire threats agin them by reason of the property which they had destroyed an' which haint been paid fer -- no, not to this day!

Hit Haint The Fish. Nat T. Winston.
1949 Southern Publishers. Kingsport, TN.

Backjaw: Insolent back-talk or sassjaw, as, "That danged game warden says to me, 'Don't give me none of yore *backjaw!*'"

* * * *

The hunting and fishing editor of the *ILLINOIS STATE JOURNAL,* Springfield, Illinois, received this letter. He could not advise the writer, could you?

* * * *

I'd like to get advice on how to reconcile two friends of mine. They are both coon hunters and, as you know, any coon hunter will fight at the least aspersion cast on the character and veracity of his favorite dog.

This fellow, Fred, trained a monkey to use with his dog and took his buddy Bill with him, one night. When his dog barked treed, they went to him and Fred unsnapped the leash on the monkey and gave him a pistol. Up the tree went the monkey. Then the pistol cracked, and down came a fat coon.

Bill said that was the most remarkable thing he had ever seen. He asked Fred if he could borrow the monkey to try him with his own dog, and Fred said he could come and get him any time, which Bill did a few nights later.

The next morning, he brought the monkey back and told Fred that the funniest thing had happened. When the dog barked treed, he gave the monkey the pistol, and the creature climbed the tree.

He stayed up the tree a long time and when he finally came down, he rushed over to the dog and shot him between the eyes — killing him dead on the spot.

Fred said that there was one thing he'd forgotten to tell Bill about that monkey. If there was anything he hated worse than a coon, it was a lying dog.

If anyone has any advice on how to get these old friends together again, I would appreciate hearing from you.

— Frank Beasley

A great story is told of the city quail hunters who stopped at a farm house to ask permission to hunt, and after visiting a while, the farmer asked it if was all right if he hunted with them. This was great with the hunters and, as they were getting the guns and dogs out of the station wagon, the farmer left and came back with his shot gun and a little, grizzly, wiry, simple-looking old man.

In answer to the hunters' questioning looks, the farmer explained that Zeke wasn't too bright, but he had a hell of a knack for locating quail. Well, sure enough, old Zeke out-hunted, out-retrieved and covered more ground than both of the high-bred pointers. In fact, they all had their limit in a couple of hours, thanks to Zeke, and the city boys could not stop talking about what an amazing hunt they had had.

The next fall these hunters showed up at the same farm. The farmer greeted them and said he had a great quail crop, and as soon as he got his gun, he was ready to go. When he came back, the anxious city hunters had their hunting coats on and guns in hand.

The farmer asked, "Where are your bird dogs?"

One hunter replied, "We didn't bring them. The way old Zeke showed them up last year, we didn't figure we would need them."

"I guess we don't hunt then," said the farmer, "I got rid of Zeke, the old fool got to catching chickens, chasing cars and howling at the moon all night, and the price of dog food just keeps going up."

GAME WARDEN, SHOOT THE S.O.B.
Harold Hoey — Marshall, MO.

✳ ✳ ✳ ✳

Like a long-tailed cat in a room full of rockin' chairs: Extreme nervousness, as, "I come sudden-like on this humongous bear. Man! I got nervous as a *long-tailed cat in a room full of rockin' chairs.*"

Consider the poetry in the description of an absolutely unneeded object: "That's about as necessary as an umbrella for a duck!"

* * * *

Two rabbits were running like crazy trying to get away from two hounds. "Wait a minute!" one rabbit yelled. "Let's stop a spell. And before they get here, we'll outnumber them!"

* * * *

It was storytelling time in the OK Saloon. One hunter started it with this one: "We were in our cabin high up in the Rockies when two enormous grizzlies starting snorting around. The other fellers all jumped out of their sleeping bags and ran for their lives. But my danged sleeping bag zipper stuck! What to do...?"

"Well, what did you do?"

"I discovered a fact I'd never known before...that it's possible to climb a tree in your sleeping bag!"

* * * *

Mess: A compliment, as, "Ol' Jake, there, he sure tells a mean story...funny as a crutch. Now ain't he a *mess!*"

* * * *

A bunch of fox-hunters waited on a hilltop, listening to the hounds chase a fox down the valley.

One native hunter said, "Ain't that the pertiest music you ever heard?"

"Yes sir! You bet. Derned if it ain't," his buddies replied.

Everyone agreed that those hounds made the prettiest music in all the world...all except a city fellow who'd come along on his first fox hunt. And he said, "I can't hear no music at all. Why, them damn dogs is making so much noise I can't hear nothin' but their damned howlin'!"

* * * *

Go to grass: A western term of disbelief, as, "How many geese did you say you killed? Ten! Aw, come on, man, you *go to grass!*"

* * * *

A farmer had left a pan of gas in the barnyard. A hunter happened by and his dog slipped through the board fence, went to the pan and lapped up the gas. Well! That dog took off lickety-split running round and round that barnlot. Ran for hours! Suddenly, the dog keeled over on its side and the hunter figured his dog was dead. But, you know, that dog wasn't dead at all...he'd just run out of gas!

* * * *

Hunky dory: Everything is fine, as, "How was huntin'?" "*Hunky dory.*"

Three hunters were bragging about how smart their dogs were. The one hunter announced that when his dog was sent for eggs, he wouldn't accept them unless they were fresh.

The second hunter said that when he sent his dog for a carton of beer, his dog would only accept his master's favorite brand. And he wouldn't take a drink until he got home and his master invited him to share the bottle. Real polite, that dog!

The third hunter said, "Them is right smart dogs you fellers got, but they can't hold a candle to mine, for smarts! Y'see, my dog owns the store where your dogs bought the beer and eggs!"

* * * *

Then there is the wife who accompanied her husband on her first deer hunting trip. She was all decked out in swell hunting clothes and looking forward to her first kill. Suddenly her husband heard a shot! He ran toward his wife, she stood with a smoking rifle in her hands.

"I must have hit something," she said with a big smile on her face. "Just listen to that language!"

* * * *

Light and set: Come and sit, as, "Git outa the boat, Pete. Come *light and set*."

* * * *

"Being a Texan and by heritage accustomed to telling the truth, I feel obligated to relate the following incident to the members of the Honest Abe Tall Tale Club.

"Several months after my arrival in Kenya to search for oil, I heard of a method used by Masai warriors for killing lions. A warrior will wrap a heavy cloth or skin about his forearm and then will take a razor-sharp knife in his other hand. When a lion attacks, the Masai will thrust his protected arm into the lion's mouth, while slitting its throat at the same time with the knife.

"This practice seemed to me to be a bit risky, so I decided to improve upon it somewhat and also capture a lion alive.

"I took a heavy towel and soaked it in a strong solution of alum and pepper for several days and started on safari.

"When I saw a huge male lion suitable to capture, I took the towel, wrapped it around my arm, and when the lion charged, thrust my arm into his mouth.

"After chewing on the towel for a second, the lion roared, started sneezing and backed off. Then the alum started to take effect and the lion's mouth puckered up so much he couldn't open it. The dose of alum was even strong enough to retract the lion's claws.

"The lion was sneezing so violently from the pepper that he couldn't run off, and as he was rendered harmless by the alum, I drew him into my Land Rover and carried him back to camp.

"Unfortunately, the lion got such an overdose of alum and pepper that he was too incapacitated to eat for weeks. He became so scrawny and mangy — by the time he could eat — that no zoo would have him. As a result I had to carry him back to the bush. Which is the only reason I do not have living proof to substantiate my story."

— David Grissett

* * * *

Precious little: A shameful few, as, "We hunted all day but killed *precious little*."

* * * *

Herb Holmes, outstanding breeder of English Pointers, asked a field trial buddy about his new dog, whether it was a setter or a pointer. The answer he got was: "He's neither one of 'em, dammit. He's a topnotch upsetter and a first class disappointer."

He got what the bear grabbed at: nothing! As, "He fired a whole lot of shells at them geese, and all *he got was what the bear grabbed at!*"

* * * *

The fish and wildlife section of the U.S. Government was ordered to study the migratory habits of birds. And so they attached the following notice, printed on metal strips, to the legs of the birds they released. The metal strips read: "Notify Fish and Wild Life Division. Wash. Biol. Surv." But they soon changed the wording after they received this penciled letter from a disappointed hunter. "Gents: I shot one of them crows ya released last week, and I followed all them silly instructions ya had on the leg. I washed it, biled it and surved it. Twasn't wuth a damn! Now y'all better quit atrying to fool folks thisaway or we'll git our senator onto ya."

* * * *

A gracious plenty: More than enough, a lot, one heluva good day's kill, as, "He killed *a gracious plenty* quail." (The opposite of "precious little.")

* * * *

Several years ago, Percy Boyer, mainstay of Middletown politics, was serving as the town clerk. A young lady of the town got a marriage license from him, allowing her to marry a Middletown lad. Only a week later she walked into the office and demanded her money back because her boyfriend had run off with a girl from Fancy Prairie.

Percy thought for a bit, then said, "Honey, I can't get you your money back. But I can do this for you...for another two bucks, I'll sell you a hunting license and you can go find him and git even."

BILL HARRISON, ARGOSY, U. S.

"When I was a young feller back in 1939," the old hunter told a bunch of young fellows down at the village store, "it got so blamed cold that you couldn't hear a sound. Sounds froze! Yep! Well, that winter I took my pack of dogs and set out to hunt rabbit. We got one up and them dogs took out after it like bolts of lightnin'. O' course, I couldn't hear anything cause all the sounds froze. And when I shot I couldn't hear no gunfire cause that sound froze, too. Well, I didn't give much thought to another strange thing...that I couldn't hear them dogs barkin' after that rabbit. Not till next spring, way after huntin' season was over, did I understand. The game warden came around and arrested me for huntin' out of season. Why? I'll tell ya why. The warden heard all that barkin' thawed out come spring, and he heard them dogs huntin' that rabbit, heard my gun go off! He arrested me for huntin' out of season."

* * * *

Shakeldy: Shakey, as, "Thet there tent of your'n is kinda *shakeldy.*"

* * * *

Smart as a tree full of owls: As, "That pointer of mine, he's *smart as a tree full of owls.*"

* * * *

A fellow from Ambrose, Tennessee, had a wonderful hunting dog, and he and his son hunted every free day they had. Well, it got time for the boy to go off to college and off he went. But he began to shoot craps and got so hooked with the game that he lost all his money. He figured out a scheme to replace it. He wrote his father: "Dear Dad, Things are going great. I'm learning a lot. And I found out that the vet school does experimental work with dogs. I told them about our dog, Old Yaller, and they said to enroll him in their program to teach dogs to read and write. So if you'll send me 200 bucks and Old Yaller, I'll enroll him." The father thought it would be great to have a dog that was literate, so he sent the dog and $200.

Well, the kid gambled away the $200, and wrote home again. "Pop, our dog is a whiz. You oughta hear him talk. And write? Well, I guess! Now they think Old Yaller so capable that they can teach him to talk. So send $400, and I'll enroll him again."

Well, the father thought it would be such fun to show the dog off before his buddies...sensational, really, that he sent the money.

Well, the kid lost the $400, and sent home, once again, for money. "Dad, Now they think they can teach Old Yaller to sing. Send another 400 bucks and we'll get started. They say he sings a mean tenor voice but needs training."

At Christmastime, the kid came home and a big bunch met the kid at the bus station because the father had spread the word about the dog and everybody wanted to see and hear Old Yaller.

"Boy, where's the dog?" the old man asked.

"Dad, wait till we get in the car. It's mighty sad, and I can't tell ya here."

"Boy, these here friends of mine have come from everywhere to see and hear Old Yaller. Now where in the hell is he?"

"In the car, Dad. Wait till we get there."

Once in the car, the boy began: "Old Yaller was doing swell, Pop, you'd of been proud. But this morning, as we were getting ready to leave for the bus and Old Yaller was reading Reader's Digest, he looked up at me and said, 'Do you reckon your Dad is still monkeyin' around with that pretty young school teacher?' I tell you, Pop, when he said that I was so derned mad that I grabbed my razor and cut his throat. He's dead."

The old man paused, cleared his throat, then said, "Son, did you make right certain he's dead?"

Laughter In Appalachia. Loyal Jones and Billy Edd Wheeler. 1987. August House, Little Rock, AK.

Poleaxe: To hit hard, to really slam the brute, as, "He *poleaxed* that derned bear and then slit his throat."

* * * *

Here's the Mike Royko of his day — our beloved Mark Twain — who was no small potato when it came to satire. Just take a look at the job he did on President Theodore Roosevelt.

THE HUNTING OF THE COW*

(October 18,1907).   Two colossal historical incidents took place yesterday, incidents which must go echoing down the corridors of time for ages, incidents which can never be forgotten while histories shall continue to be written. Yesterday, for the first time, business was opened to commerce by the Marconi Company and wireless messages sent entirely across the Atlantic, straight from shore to shore; and on that same day the President of the United States for the fourteenth time came within three miles of flushing a bear. As usual he was far away, nobody knew where, when the bear burst upon the multitude of dogs and hunters and equerries and chamberlains in waiting, and sutlers and cooks and scullions, and Rough Riders and infantry and artillery, and had his customary swim to the other side of the pond and disappeared in the woods. While half the multitude watched the place where he vanished, the other half galloped off, with horns blowing, to scour the state of Louisiana in search of the great hunter. Why don't they stop hunting the bear altogether and hunt the President? He is the only one of the pair that can't be found when he is wanted.

By and by the President was found and laid upon the track and he and the dogs followed it several miles through the woods, then gave it up, because Rev. Dr. Long, the "nature fakir," came along and explained that it was a cow track. This is a sorrowful ending to a mighty enterprise. His Excellency leaves for Washington today, to interest himself further in his scheme of provoking a war in Japan with his battleships...

(October 21, 1907). Alas, the President has got that cow after all! If it was a cow. Some say it was a bear — a real bear. These were eyewitnesses, but they were all White House domestics; they are all under wages to the great hunter, and when a witness is in that condition it makes his testimony doubtful. The fact that the President himself thinks it was a bear does not diminish the doubt but enlarges it. He was once a reasonably modest man, but his judgment has been out of focus so long now that he imagines that everything he does, little or big, is colossal.

I am sure he honestly thinks it was a bear, but the circumstantial evidence that it was a cow is overwhelming. It acted just as a cow would act when in trouble; it even left a cow track behind, which is what a cow would do when in distress, or indeed at any other time if it knew a President of the United States was after it — hoping to move his pity, you see; thinking maybe he would spare her life on account of her sex, her helpless situation, and her notorious harmlessness. In her flight she acted just as a cow would have done when in a frenzy of fright, with a President of the United States and a squadron of dogs chasing after her; when her strength was exhausted, and she could drag herself no further, she did as any other despairing cow would have done — she stopped in an open spot, fifty feet wide, and humbly faced the President of the United States with the tears running down her cheeks, and said to him with the mute eloquence of surrender: "Have pity, sir, and spare me. I am alone, you are many; I have no weapon but my helplessness, you are a walking arsenal; I am in awful peril, you are as safe as you would be in a Sunday school; have pity, sir — there is no heroism in killing an exhausted cow."

In the outcome the credit is all with the cow, none of it is with the President. When the poor hunted thing could go no further it turned, in fine and picturesque defiance, and gallantly faced its enemies and its assassin. From a safe distance Hercules sent a bullet to the sources of its life; then, dying, it made fight — so was a hero present after all. Another bullet closed the tragedy, and Hercules was so carried away with admiration of himself that he hugged his domestics and bought a compliment from one of them for twenty dollars.

From *Mark Twain's Memoirs*

* * * *

Now here's a doggone good tail.

"I am in the Air Force, stationed in the fabulous coon country around Waco, Texas. When I first arrived here, I got a coon dog to top all dogs. He could even track a coon across a running river.

"A strange thing happened, though, one day. My dog up and died. Even the vets couldn't tell me the cause of his death.

"I had loved that dog so much I wanted something to remind me of him, so I had a taxidermist make a pair of moccasins from his hide.

"Shortly after this, I was walking in a field one day, wearing those moccasins, when they hit a coon trail — and I'll tell you, those shoes ran me five miles before I could shake them."

— Etton Newsome. ARGOSY MAGAZINE

* * * *

Cut across lots: To leave hurriedly, as, "He took one sniff of that skunk and then he *cut across lots* and ain't got back yet." (Recorded as early as 1850 — and still used!)

* * * *

Here's a bit more of that inimitable 19th century humorist, Josh Billings. *It was great fun, back then, to spell words the way they sounded. Well, even today it is a good idea...and funny, too. Now, doesn't it make sense to spell enough, as "enuff"; and has, as "haz"; and is, as "iz"; and to, as "tew"?

THE QUAIL

The quail iz a game bird, about one size bigger than the robin, and so sudden that they hum when they fly.

They hav no song, but whissell for musik; the tune iz solitary and sad.

They are shot on the wing, and a man may be good in arithmetick, fust rate at parseing, and even be able tew preach acceptably, but if he hain't studdied quail on the wing, he might az well shoot at a streak ov lightning in the sky az at a quail on the go.

Briled quail, properly supported with jellys, toast, and a champane Charlie, iz just the most diffikult thing, in mi humble opinyun, to beat in the whole history ov vittles and sumthing tew drink.

I am no gourmand, for i kan eat bred and milk five days out ov seven, and smak my lips after i git thru, but if i am asked to eat briled quail by a friend, with judishious accompanyments, i blush at fust then bow mi hed, and then smile sweet acquiescence — in other words, I always quail before such a request.

✳ ✳ ✳ ✳

THE SNIPE

The snipe is a gray, misterious bird, who git up out ov low, wet places quick, and git back again quick.

They are pure game, and are shot on the move.

They are az tender tew brile az a saddle rok oyster, and eat az eazy az sweetmeats.

The snipe haz a long bill (about the length ov a doktor's) and git a living by thrusting it down into the fat earth, and then pumping the juices out with their tounge.

I hav seen snipe so phatt that when they waz shot 50 feet in the air and phell on to the hard ground, they would split open like an egg.

This will sound like a lie to a man who never haz seen it did, but after he haz seen it did, he will feel different about it.

THE PARTRIDGE

The partridge is a kind ov wild hen, and liv in the swamps, and on the hill sides that are woody.

They are verry eazy tew ketch with the hand, if yu kan git near enuff tew them tew put salt on their tale, but this iz al-wus diffikult for nu beginners.

In the spring ov the year they will drum a tune with their wings on some deserted old log, and if yu draw ni unto them tew observe the musik, they will rize up, and kut a hole thru the air with a hum like a bullet.

Thare iz no burd kan beat a partridge on the wing for one hundred yards, i am authorized tew bet on this.

The partridge are a game burd, and are shot on the wing, if they are not missed.

It iz dreadful natral tew miss a partridge on the fly, especially if a tree gets in the way.

I hav hunted a grate deal for partridge, and lost a grate deal ov time at it.

The partridge lays 14 eggs, and iz az sure tew hatch all her eggs out az a cockroach iz who feels well.

When a brood ov yung partridges fust begin tew toddle about with the old bird, they look like a lot ov last year's chestnut burs on legs.

Broiled partridge iz good if yu kan git one that waz born during the present century, but thare iz a grate menny partridge around that waz with Noah in the ark, and they are az tuff tew git the meat oph ov az a hoss shu.

But broiled partridge iz better than broiled krow, and i had rather hav broiled krow than broiled mule just for a change.

Partridges are shot on the wing, and are az easy to miss az a ghost iz.

It iz phun enuff to see the old bird hide her yung brood when danger iz near. This must be seen, it kant be described and make enny boddy beleave it.

The partridge, grouse, and pheasant are cousins, and either one ov them straddle a gridiron natural enuff tew hav bin born thare.

THE WOODKOK

The woodkok iz one ov them kind ov birds who kan git up from the ground with about az much whizz, and about az bizzy az a fire-kracker, and fly away az krooked az a korkscrew.

They feed on low, wet lands, and only eat the most delikate things.

They run their tungs down into the soft earth, and gather tender juices and tiny phood.

They have a long, slender bill, and a rich brown plumage, and when they lite on the ground yu lose sight ov them az quick az yu do ov a drop ov water when it falls into a mill pond.

The fust thing yu generally see ov a woodkok is a whizz, and the last thing a whurr.

How so many ov them are killed on the wing iz a mistery to me, for it iz a quicker job than snatching pennys oph a red-hot stove.

I hav shot at them often, but i never heard ov my killing one ov them yet.

They are one ov the game birds, and menny good judges think they are the most elegant vittles that wear feathers.

* A superb collection of Josh Billings' views on life and living is available.
Title: *AMERICA'S PHUNNIEST PHELLOW — JOSH BILLINGS.* Hardback: $14.95. Softback: $7.95 Order from Lincoln-Herndon Press. 818 South Dirksen Parkway, Springfield, Illinois 62703

* * * *

Didn't know straight up: Confused, as, "I was lost so bad, for so long, I got so I *didn't know straight up.*"

* * * *

Pete Edwards had wanted to go on an African Safari all of his life. Finally, the opportunity came along and Pete left for Africa. Nobody heard from him for six weeks, and then he showed up at his hometown where everyone asked him how he had enjoyed the safari.

Pete was unenthusiastic and non-committal. A friend asked him to tell about his experience.

"Oh, it was all right, I guess. Not bad."

"Only ordinary, Pete? I'm surprised," his friend said. "You didn't get chased by a lion? Or run up a tree by a leopard? Or shot at by a tribesman?"

"Well, this one thing happened and it was kind of unusual..."

"So tell me about it."

"Well, my friend Earnest had a very strange experience."

"What was that?"

"I'll just let him tell you," Pete said. He reached in his pocket and pulled out a small box. A man about three inches tall stepped out. "Earnest, old buddy, tell my friend what you said to that witch doctor that got him so mad at you."

* * * *

Folks in cloisters
Should not eat oysters!

* * * *

Chance: Quantity, as, "I got me a smart *chance* of ducks, yesterday."

* * * *

The avid field trialer was bitten in three places by his favorite English pointer. He rushed to the doctor, who checked the dog, and reported that the fellow would probably get rabies and should immediately be inoculated against it.

The bitten hunter took out a pen and paper and began to write.

"No need for a will, sir," the doctor assured him. "The vaccination will remove the danger."

"I understand you, Doc, but first I want to make some quick notes on who I want to bite, before you cure me."

Two Sangamon County, Illinois hunters were far afield looking for quail when they heard a distant church bell ringing just before dark.

"By gosh, that's the church bell. I forgot there was a prayer meeting tonight."

"I couldn't have gone," his buddy said. "My wife's too sick."

* * * *

Skin hunter: A man who hunts for pelt, for fur, for profit.

* * * *

There's an ancient story floating around about a hunter with an old buffalo gun. He shot a deer, shot only once, hit the deer in the head and also tore off one of his hind feet.

When asked how it was that he could hit the deer in the head and still tear off the hindfoot, the hunter replied, "Now, boys 'twasn't the size of the bullet. They's big, all right, but they ain't that big. But it so happened that the deer he was ascratchin' his ear with his hind foot so that when I hit his head I hit his foot, too. Now, boys, that's the gospel truth."

* * * *

Back in the old days, a fellow in Macon County, Illinois, bought a mule from a mighty sharp horse-trader. The trader told this fellow that, "Thiseyer mule'll p'int quail same as a bird dog. Yessir she'll jest squat right down and go to pointin' a covey, good as any dog."

So the fellow buys the mule and rides it toward home. He had to cross the Sangamon River to get to his home but, halfway across, that blamed mule squatted down and the fellow got soaked. So he took the mule back to the trader and demanded his money back.

"Oh, shucks, I plumb forgot to tell ya. Thet wonderful mule there...he points fish, too."

* * * *

Quail: A pretty, sexy young girl or woman.

This fellow had a hunting dog that he boasted was the smartest dog in the world.

"Why, that dog of mine has got more intelligence than half the people."

Of course, everyone laughed at such a ridiculous statement. But the fellow went on: "Just listen to this, you guys, and see if I'm not right. Two weeks ago my house caught fire. All of us began to carry stuff out, stuff that wasn't worth much, like dishes, books and things like that. But do you know what my dog did? He went into that house — after the rest of us were smoked out and he came back with a piece of paper in his mouth. And that paper, fellows, was my fire insurance policy."

* * * *

Javeline: A wild pig that is said to resemble "A ball of hair with a butcher knife through it."

* * * *

ANOTHER BEAR FIGHT
by "Ruff Sam" of Mississippi

This story about a backwoodsman from Mississippi appeared in the popular sporting newspaper, **Spirit of the Times**, on March 4, 1848.

I'm rite from the backwoods of Mississippi, and as I told you onct 'bout my fite at Bony Vista.[1] The folks have been pesterin me to death to tell em sumthin of the bar an panther hunts I've had, how many I kilt and wether I was kilt or no, 'twill I've gis' determined to tell em of a rale swingin hunt I had last October.

You see, I left these parts in Ceptember and went strate hum. I arriv thar, and arter shakin hans with all the wimin folkes and kissin all the galls, the boys raised a bar hunt, and nuthin would do but I must go 'long. Thar was Bill Beenyard and Long Jim — but thar is no use in givin names for you doesn't know em — depend on it, thar was a parcel on em. We all got reddy at Squire Startises at the forks of the road, kalkulatin we'd start out next mornin by crack of day. Sure nuff next morning kum — I shuck

1. Battle of Buena Vista. Mexican War, 1846-1848

myself an got out in the yard, kummenced blowin for the dogs. The other boys hain't much usen to huntin, so they was snorin 'bout that time. I blowed agin and here kum the dogs a-howlin and wagin thar tales, an a-lookin so eager — but I hadn't orter sed that Boss was a-wagin his tale cause he got it bit off onct by a darned old she-tiger cat, an tain't never growed out yit. The boys kum a-stretchin themselves and axed me what all fired thunder that was. You see they hearn my horn and took it for thunder — I'm prodeegeous on a wind insterment an I sorter skeered em — but I insured em it wouldn't rain nor nuthin, and everything bein fixed off we put. They wanted me to go long with the krowd, but I wasn't goin to do nuthin of the kind, so I tole em they'd fine me at the big bend in the kreek and then struck for the kanebrake.

Thar hain't never been a place yit whar Ruff Sam kouldn't git throo. I whistled for Boss and gin him a few injunkshuns, such as "Look him up, sir-r-r!" "Mind what you 'bout, you bob-taled raskel!" — sorter urgin of him on — didn't mean to hurt his feelins, and he noed it. You ort to ha' seen him — Lord, how he riggled himself — a-camellin on the groun' — a-kockin his ears, a-histenin his tale, and a-whinin an cuttin setch numbersome kapers that you'd ha' thot he had tread in a wass ness. He seed I wasn't arter no turkeys nor deer for he never let on he noticed em.

We had pushed throo 'bout a mile of kane break when I began to feel a varmint of sum sort nigh me, and Boss felt him too. 'Twas powerful dark — the sun wasn't more an up, and it didn't stan' no chance for the kane, 'twas so 'mazin thick.

"What is ail you, you skoundrel?" sez I, a-turnin roun to Boss.

Thar he stood, his legs spraddled out and his grizzly sides a-swellin in an out like a pair of bellewes.

"What on airth is the matter?" sez I, a-gittin mad — I patted him on the back an a-coaxed him; 'twant no use — he wouldn't budge.

That made me rale feerce and rip, rip, diff! I gin it to him in the ribs with my fist shet up.

"Now, what ails you?" sez I.

Boss looked at me an said, jest as plane as a dog kin say, he was skeered. I know'd sumthin most orful was kummin, or Boss would never ha' been skeered. I stopped and considered, an I mout ha' taken a little sumthin what I have 'long in a goard, but I won't say I did. I studdied on an speclated and I mout ha' taken a nuther drop or so, but I won't swar to it, I looks at Boss, and sez, "Boss, is you goin to foller me, or is you not?" He wanted to sodger out of the skrage, an I seed it in him; his har was stanin strate out all over him. Sez I, "If it's a whale you shall fite him, you kowardly Mexikin raskil!" You must ha' knowed I was savage, or I never would a-called my dog a Mexikin! Suddenly I hearn sumthin, and turnin I seed one of the most stonishin big she bars that ever wored fur standin afore me, within ten foot. When she seed me a-lookin at her she grunted, as much as to say, "Who's afeered!" Sez I, "Say your prayers quick; I wants your hide!" and lets drive with my rifle. Jest as I fired she throed her head round, an it took her in the shoulder. That riled her tremendious, and she kum at me afore I kould say who's who. I looked round and seed Boss a-watchin on close by, jest as the kritter closed in with me. "Charge her in the rair!" I shouted out to Boss. Zip! I kum down with the butt end of my rifle, smashin it to pieces. She shuck her head an grabbed for me; but feelin the enimy a-worryin her in the rair, she wheeled. That gin me time to git out my old bowie knife, and I flanked her with it rale quick. She manoovered an kum to the charge agin in the bilin swet, bitin an showin fite in dead airnest. I was a-fallin back for a new position as my foot slipped, an kefetchup! I kum on my back! I thot the thing was out then an kommenced thinkin 'bout kingdom kum. She got me in her arms rale sure nuff, an if you say she didn't squeeze me, you doesn't know nuthin tall 'bout it. I tried to breathe, but the wind in me was so skase I kouldn't. She hugged me so tite that my fingers got as strate as stix; my head begin to swell 'bout the size of a whisky barl, an I sorter thot I mite bust or brake or sumthin if she presd me much harder. Presently I hearn her a-tremblin, and then she loosend her holt an rolled over on her side. I laid still 'twill I got to my usual size and then riz up to look for Boss. I was willin to quit. Thar was Boss, one of the bisiest dogs you ever seed, a-findin what she was made outen — he naterally had his head clane in the hole I had made in her with old bowie. The bar was dead, an me an Boss had licked her!

I was a-skinnin of her when the boys kum up, an sech a nuther spree we had arter we got to the Squire's I never spects to have agin.

"EITHER STOP CRITICISING OR COME UP HERE AND LEAD!"

Prosperity: If you see a rabbit and no one is chasing him, times ain't too bad.

** ** ** **

A group of hunters were discussing their dogs. They asked Jake, an excellent coon hunter, how he liked his new dog.

"Fine, just fine," Jake said. "Moves good, great style, tireless. But he does have one fault."

"What's that, Jake?"

"He follows coon tracks just fine...but backwards!"

* * * *

A MORALITY TALE

A lion escaped from the circus and wandered through the countryside. Suddenly, he came upon a herd of cows. He killed the bull and ate it, horns, hoofs and hide. That bull made such a great meal that the lion roared and roared his satisfaction. The farmer heard him roar, grabbed his gun, ran to the pasture, saw the lion and shot him dead. The moral: When you are full of bull, keep your mouth shut.

* * * *

Duck-fit: A horrendous fit of anger, as, "He took him a real *duck-fit* when I told him he couldn't go huntin' with us."

* * * *

A bunch of hunters were sitting around the tavern. They had just finished a weekend of good hunting and were discussing their luck.

"I came to this huge oak tree," the one hunter began. "And there on one huge limb sat 100 squirrels. What a break. So I took careful aim and killed 99 of 'em. Damned if I didn't."

"Hey, man," another hunter kidded him. "Couldn't you make that an even hundred squirrels so's we'd have a nice, round, even number?"

"What kind of a man do you think I am! Do you think I'd lie for the sake of one measly damned squirrel?"

* * * *

Two greenhorns decided they would learn how to hunt quail. So they bought a very expensive bird dog and took him to the field. After working the dog for half the day, they were thoroughly disgusted. "By gosh, George, this dog ain't worth a damn. I'm going to shoot the sonovagun."

"Let's try him one more time, Eddie," the other cautioned. "Let's not be so danged hasty. You throw him up in the air one more time and if the sucker don't fly then, well, we'll go get our money back."

* * * *

Rabbit: A salad consisting entirely of green, leafy vegetables.

* * * *

A quail took off with a whir of feathers, flying away from two hunters. Both missed him. But when that quail got back to his nesting grounds, he was a mess. He was missing half his feathers. His beak was broken! One leg dangled so limply and he could barely open one eye.

"Did you get shot at, dear?" his mate asked.

"Yeah! But I got away from those two guys. They couldn't shoot worth a hoot."

"Then what happened? You're a mess!" said the lady quail.

"I was flying too low and got caught in a badminton game."

* * * *

Eddie and Joe were a bit light in the upper story or, as they say, about half a pint short of a quart! They went hunting one day and didn't see any game.

About mid-afternoon, Eddie said, "Joe, let's go on for another hour and then go home."

Joe agreed. They walked on and came to an open spot in the forest. Lo and behold! A gal was sitting there...plumb naked. She waved them over to her.

Joe said, "Honey, are you game?" She grins and says, "You bet I am."

So Eddie ups and shoots her!

Seems like some fellows can't tell a story without getting mixed up. But maybe old Ebenezer wasn't all that confused.

It seems that old Eben, as they called him, was out berrying one fine June day. He came across a bear. So Eben turns and begins to run like crazy, uphill and down and across the country. Finally, he came to the Illinois River.

"Well, sir," says Eben, "I crossed that river on thick ice and the bear didn't follow."

"Come on, now, Eben. It was June. How come there was ice on the Illinois in June?"

"Well, boys, I done a heap of runnin'. A whole heap. And by this time 'twas the middle of January."

* * * *

Bear: A first-rate person or thing. A humdinger, as, "He's a *bear*!"

* * * *

Those same two fellows, Eddie and Joe...you remember them...the ones half a pint short of a quart...well, they went deer-hunting. They agreed that if one of them got lost while separated from the other, the one who was lost would fire three shots and wait for the other to rescue him. Well, Joe got lost. He fired three shots and waited. Eddie didn't show up. So he fired three more shots and still no Eddie.

So he began to walk, and after a bit, he ran into Eddie.

"How come you didn't come to find me when I was lost?" Joe asked.

"Did you fire three shots?"

"Sure. Twice I done it. But I only had one arrow left after that, so I started walkin'!"

* * * *

Pete had a new friend, Eddie, who owned a bird dog that he claimed could not only find and point birds but count how many birds were in the covey. So Pete and

Eddie went hunting. Of course, Pete didn't really believe that any dog could do all that, but he almost became a believer when the dog came runnin' back, scratched the ground six times, went back and pointed a covey of six quail!

After they worked the covey, the dog took off again, and this time he came back and scratched the ground nine times. They followed him and, sure enough, there were nine birds in the covey.

"That's just normal for my dog," Eddie said. So they worked those birds and the great dog took off again only to come back and start hunching his master's leg.

"Uh-huh! I knew that dog couldn't really count," Pete said, "that it was all a fake! But tell me...why in the hell is he humping your leg?"

"Like I told you," Eddie replied, "he's one smart dog. He's telling me that there's a covey out there that's just too fuckin' big for him to count."

Stomach SOS: Hunger, as, "Let's quit huntin' and get on back to camp for vittles. I got me a genuine *stomach SOS.*"

* * * *

There was an old hunter who had wounded a mallard duck. He took him home, took such a fancy to that duck that he couldn't kill him, so he made a pet of him. Well, that duck went everywhere with the old man. One day, the old fellow decided to go to the movies. He couldn't bear to leave that duck at home. But to stop any complaints from the management, he put the duck in his pants where nobody could see it. He bought a ticket and sat down. Everything was fine, the movie was good and the old fellow forgot about the duck. Suddenly, he remembered and opened his zipper so that the duck could get some fresh air.

Two little old ladies were sitting next to him and one turned to the other and said, "Marybelle, the old man sitting next to me just unzipped his britches."

Her sister replied, "Oh, sister, for you that's nothing new. You've seen it before."

The other said, "Yes, but this one is eating my popcorn."

* * * *

Moose milk: Whiskey!

* * * *

A farmer discovered that two squirrels were stealing a lot of corn out of his crib. It seems that they nested in a big hollow tree near the crib from which they stole corn. So, one day, when the squirrels were in the crib getting corn, the farmer cut down the tree and removed it. He came back with his shotgun, shot into the crib, scared the squirrels out and they scampered quick as lightning to the tree and climbed up so fast that they were sixty feet in the air before they realized that the tree wasn't there!

A WILDCAT STORY
by Anonymous of Louisiana

The following tale appeared in the **Spirit of the Times**, XX, No. 13 (May 18, 1850), 148, reprinted from the **New Orleans Picayune**.

Many years ago in the wilds of the western part of Mississippi, there lived an old hunter by the name of Rube Fox, who was as notorious in that section of country as ever Martin Scott was in the West.

One day Rube came down with a small party of friends to take a hunt on Deer Creek, and they stopped at the house of a widow, who occasionally took in travellers to stay all night. Rube was a very stout, athletic man, about six feet two inches in height, and wore his hair and beard very long. His cheeks, nose, and upper lip were deeply scarred, which gave him a very savage appearance. The widow had often "hearn tell on Rube" but had never seen him, and when he entered the room of the log house and put his rifle down in the corner, she curtsied and said, "Mr. Fox, I believe." "You believe right," said Rube, "your sarvant, marm."

After supper, which consisted of fried and stewed "bar meat," the widow, who had been listening to Rube telling hunting stories and had watched his curious countenance, was suffering all the tortures of an anxious curiosity to find out what had scarred his face. She could hold in no longer, and at last puckering up her mouth she said, "I reckon, Mr. Fox, you got them scars on your face in the canebrake."

"No, I didn't, marm," replied Rube with a scowl which was a first-rate imitation of the look of a hyena.

This sorter dampened the old lady, but the spirit of Mother Eve was too strong in her to give it up so. "If you got it in a fight," said the old lady with a sly look of malice, "I didn't mean to rile you by askin 'bout it."

"I ain't riled," said Rube, trying to smile but looking more like a man who was suddenly taken with a severe twinge of the colic. "But it warn't in a fight, old lady," said Rube, as well as his friends, appeared to enjoy mightily the widow's curiosity.

"Well, if it warn't in a fight, and it's not imparlite to ask you," said the widow screwing up all her energy to the task, "how did you get them upper scars?" Rube shoved up his upper lip and moved it from one side to the other in a way he had while the little party could hardly keep in from laughing outright. Turning to the widow he said "Well, marm, I got these scars by lookin whar I hadn't ought to."

This was too much. The widow crimsoned, and the party burst into a loud laugh.

"Come, Rube," said one of his friends, "tell the story."

"It's no story," said Rube, "but an ugly fact. My neighborhood had been affected for some time in the chicken line, and their disappearance could not be accounted for until one day I got on the track of a big wildcat. As the ground was very damp I trailed up the varmint till I got nearly on him, when I brought my rifle up to my cheek — "

"And it burst," cried the widow.

"No, it didn't," continued Rube with another of his looks, "the blasted gun snapped, misfired and the cat sprung to a tree, which was hollow at the fork, and crept into the hole. The cunnin of the thing vexed me so I swore I'd come it over her anyhow; so I tuck to the tree and climbed up to the fork. I drew my knife to cut a limb so as to worry the cat out. As soon as I got fixed, I put my face down to the hollow of the fork to look into the hole. I saw two balls of fire and heard a growl. The blasted varmint had her young thar, and afore I could draw back my head she nearly grabbed me in the face with her claws. The thing took me so unawares that I let go all holds and fell about forty feet to the ground, and if you ever catch me going wildcat huntin again, I wish I may be eternally and everlastingly — eh," and here Rube moved his upper lip again as his eye caught that of the widow's

"No, I didn't either," said Rube.

"Then, how on airth was it?" asked the widow, catching a long breath and becoming so excited that she could hardly sit still.

"Well, you see, I never rightly knew," said Rube winking to the boys, "but they used to tell it that dad and mammy fit one day and she scratched him pretty badly, and I was born with the scars."

* * * *

Maybe all hunters should cultivate a handlebar moustache, like this Marine?

"I want to set all the quail hunters straight on my secret way of putting quail on the menu. The advantages of my system are ease of execution and no shot-up birds to clean, as well as no monetary outlay for guns and ammo. Being a Marine, I am just naturally honest — so you can be sure this is a true story.

"Having worn a handlebar mustache much of my life, I never realized its full value until a couple of years ago.

"I was on an extended hunt, hike and exploration trip, out in the wilds of New Mexico. During this trip, I did not trim my mustache.

"My little bird dog, Trixie, was with me and she is as smart as a whip. When I spotted a large covey of quails in front of me, I sent Trixie around the right flank to run them back toward me. She ran them a little too fast, and the birds flushed.

"I was surprised to see them all fly straight toward me, and I stood very still. Those birds lit in my huge mustache, and the weight almost pulled me to the ground. They thought my mustache was a bush.

"I put my head into a burlap sack and shook it, and the quail fell off my mustache. I kept the legal limit and released the others, as I am a law-abiding sportsman."

— D.A. Schott
ARGOSY MAGAZINE, reprinted by permission of
Argosy Communications, Inc. © 1990

* * * *

There's a new way to catch rabbits. They developed the system in Missouri. Yes sir, hard to believe, but that's where the system was invented. Here's how it goes. You lay some cabbage leaves beside and close to a big rock. Then you sprinkle some pepper on the leaves. When the rabbit starts to eat the cabbage, he starts to sneeze, and the sneeze-action causes him to butt his head against the rock.

He knocks himself unconscious, and that's when you hurry over, pick him up and stuff him in your game bag. The system is called: CAUGHT BETWEEN A LEAF AND A HARD PLACE.

* * * *

Doodly squat: Insignificant, trivial, as, "It don't make me no mind! It don't mean *diddly (or doodly) squat.*"

* * * *

There are a lot of tall tales about killing multiple game with only one shot, and they go back hundreds of years. One appeared earlier. Here is another, a true (?) one. It seems this South Dakota guy went hunting and roused him a big bear. He took a quick shot at the bear, and that bullet went in one side of the bear, out the other and on to hit a deer just beyond. Now, the blast from the gun caused the fellow to fall off the perch he was sitting on, and he landed on a covey of quail and killed them all. Not only that, but the fall dislodged a button off his pants, and that button shot on and killed a rabbit. Why, that fellow had meat all winter from that one shot.

* * * *

Joe Jones, an enthusiastic fox hunter, bought a horse from shrewd, old trader Eddie Peters. As soon as Jones got his new horse in his stable, the animal lay down and died. Since Joe was a mighty powerful citizen, as soon as Eddie Peters heard the bad news, he left the area for parts unknown.

Peters came back to town some two years later and happened to run into Joe Jones before he could avoid contact. So he did what any trader would do, he begged Joe's pardon and offered to do what was fair to recompense Joe for the dead horse.

"Don't let that worry you for one minute, Eddie," Joe said as friendly as could be. "That hoss made me five thousand bucks. As soon as the sucker died, I kept it still as night and offered raffle tickets on the horse, a buck a ticket, and I had six thousand buyers."

"All well and good," said the trader Eddie Peters, "but what did you tell the guy that won the raffle?"

Joe grinned. "Well, I told him the truth, that the horse had died, and I gave him his money back plus a wee bit extra for the inconvenience of the thing. So everybody was happy, especially me."

✳   ✳   ✳   ✳

Two guys were hunting bear out in Wyoming. Suddenly they came upon a big, black sucker who looked like an entire winter's meat supply. Both men aimed and fired, only wounding the bear who started toward them, hell bent for election. The one guy quickly grabbed a pair of running shoes out of his pack.

"Man, come on!" his buddy shouted. "You ain't got time to put on them things and outrun that bear."

"I don't have to outrun him, I only got to outrun you!"

✳   ✳   ✳   ✳

As welcome as a collect telegram: Something as joyous as getting chiggers up your pants-leg on a hot summer's day!

✳   ✳   ✳   ✳

They tell the story about a Kentuckian who had a prize fox and raccoon dog. This fellow, like most Kentuckians, held that dog in the highest esteem, treasured his welfare above almost any other critter in the world, not excluding his own family!

One day he was putting up hay when a rabbit got up in front of the hay wagon. The dog jumped down and took off after that rabbit, but the Kentuckian called sharply for him to come back and, "git up in thiseyer wagon." The dog obeyed and then the man, himself, took off, chasing the same rabbit. He came back wringin' wet and out of breath.

"How come you didn't sic your hound on that rabbit? Why'd you call him back?" his helper asked.

"You plumb nuts? Whatever give you the notion that I'd allow a great ol' dog like him to run himself ragged in heat like this?"

There's a revealing fox-hunter story about a bunch of Kentuckians who were crazy about fox hunting. They were at it all night. Had a great old time, too. Returning home, they watched the sun come up. Just then a bunch of fishermen passed them. One of the fox hunters exclaimed, "What on earth would possess a man to be silly enough to get up and go fishing this early in the morning?"

Bearcat: Something superior, admirable, first-rate, as, "When Eddie goes after quail, he always comes back with his limit. He's a *bearcat* hunter!"

* * * *

A field trialer approached the reservation desk at a hotel near the field trial grounds. He asked the attendant if his dog could share the room.

The attendant looked the field trialer over from head to foot and replied, "I've been in this business for twenty-five years, and I never yet had to call the police to eject a drunk and disorderly dog at four in the morning. And what's more, I've never had a dog give me a bad check or start a fire in his room while smoking in bed. And I have never, never discovered in a dog's suitcase one or more of our hotel towels. So, by all means, your pointer can stay. He's welcome. And, if he'll vouch for you, you can stay, too."

* * * *

A newspaper's super-dooper-blooper:

"That hunting and fishing are good in Colorado is shown by the fact that of 100,000 hunters out during the recent game season there were 80,000 killed. This is a record that cannot be equalled in the United States."

— Colorado newspaper

* * * *

Two duck hunters were having a few beers in the local tavern. The one guy was moaning and groaning about the way his wife bawled him out for spending so much time hunting. "And that ain't all," he went on, "sometimes she deliberately refuses to cook supper unless I agree to stay home weekends. And sometimes she..."

"I know. I know," his buddy replied. "My advice to you is to go home tonight and show her who's boss. Tell her off! Demand she cook meals three times a day, and the food you like! Demand it! Y'understand?"

"I sure do. And I'll do it," his buddy said, grinning at the pleasure he was about to enjoy when he got home.

The timid husband jogged home, rehearsing exactly what he would do and say so that when he entered his home, he was ready. "Mabel, by God, from here on I'm taking no more of your guff. You'll have my meals on time! And tonight I want supper ready in ten minutes. Got that? And get out my best clothes because I'm goin' back and have some fun with my buddies tonight. And do you know who is goin' to help select them clothes and see that I'm dressed right?" He leered at her.

"Yep! I sure do," his wife replied. "The undertaker!"

* * * *

A woman hunter was about to fire when her husband restrained her.

"Don't worry, dear," she assured him. "I'm sure it's OK. I distinctly heard that moose moo."

* * * *

A New Yorker was out in the woods with his bird dog, hunting partridge. It was a successful day. Nearing the end of it, the hunter headed back to his car only to find that it would not start. He wasn't too far from a small town so he headed that way where he and his dog waited for the bus.

But, when the bus arrived, the conductor looked at the man and his dog and said, "Mister, you can't get on this bus!"

"Why not? My car won't start. I need to get back to New York."

"No dogs allowed on this bus, Buddy!"

"What the hell are you telling me!" the hunter yelled. "You mean that me and my dog can't ride with you?"

"Nope. You can. Not your dog."

"All right. But you know what you can do with your godamned bus!"

The driver nodded, then replied, "You do the same with your dog and you can get on the bus!"

Puns and hunting are about as compatible as milk and vinegar! But, once in a while, a hunting pun appears that bears (just barely) repeating. Consider this one.

Q. What did the New Yorker say when he shot a deer that had been born eyeless?

A. I have no eye deer.

* * * *

Drove up: Extremely busy, as, "I'm too *drove up* to go huntin' today."

* * * *

An experienced hunter had his friend along, but the friend had never been hunting. They were in a blind waiting for a skein of geese. Finally, one showed up and the experienced guy blasted away. Two ducks fell to the water.

"Pretty good shot I made, eh, buddy?"

"Not bad. Not bad."

"Whadaya mean, 'not bad.' Hell, man, those two shots were terrific."

"Oh, I don't know...seems like the fall alone woulda killed 'em."

There was a sign, not at all unusual, posted near a farm fence along a country road. It read: NO HUNTING. Now, that wasn't so unusual, but what was written below it was: "YOU'RE TELLING ME!"

* * * *

Deer hunter: "Nice farm you got here, and I'd sure like to hunt deer. Would you allow me to do that?"

Farmer: "Yep. But be mighty careful not to shoot at nothin' that don't move. Likely, it'd be my hired man."

* * * *

Hunting: Noise with discipline!

* * * *

During the recent national arguments for and against fur coats, a couple — very much against using fur for clothing — visited a well-known mink farm. They asked the owner if they might look around, and he agreed to accompany them on their rounds.

Very soon the owner got the idea that the visiting couple were among those opposed to using animal fur for clothing.

When they paused before a pen of live mink, the lady asked, "How many times a year do you skin them?"

The owner was prepared. "Just the one time ma'am. 'Cause if you skin 'em more than once, they jist git meaner'n hell!"

* * * *

Not many know about it, but back in the early days, out in the far west, the hunters and trappers were so tough they used chewed-off shotguns!

* * * *

The Lands and Forests Department of the state of Ontario has a useful bulletin dealing with the porcupine. It goes as follows:

"The best way to effect his capture is to wait until he's in the open. Then, watching for his slapping tail, rush in quickly and pop a large washtub over him. In this way you have a good seat to rest on while you try to figure out what to do next."

* * * *

Did you hear about the first-time hunter, a real dingbat who, the night before the hunt and during a crap game, refused to shoot craps with his buddies?
He said, "I don't know how to cook them!"

* * * *

A group of first-time hunters were coming back to camp after their first day's shoot. They had paid dearly for their inexperience! One guy's hand was in a sling; another was hopping around on one foot; and a third looked like he'd been a in dog fight.
"So don't worry about it, fellows," reassured an old timer, "from the bulge in your bag you must have had a darned good day in the field. By gosh, you aren't coming back skunked."
The fellow holding the bag said, "That's our hunting dog."

* * * *

Longer'n a hard winter: Endless, as, "That jo-jeezly game warden lectured me *longer'n a hard winter.*"

* * * *

A bunch of hunters had a wonderful but timid cook back at the base camp. They tried for days to get him to come along with them during the hunting excitement, but he always refused. Finally, he agreed to go with them.
"But," he cautioned them, "if you gits to wrestling with that big grizzly you is after, and you looks around and you don't see a soul, well, that's me."

* * * *

A hunter walks into a bar with his dog and orders two martinis, one for himself, the other for the dog. The bartender thinks this is kind of strange, but he obliges the guy, puts a martini in front of him and one before the dog.

Both the dog and the man empty their glasses, eat the olives, chew up the glasses and then spit out the stems.

This goes on for three more drinks! The guy looks at the bartender and says, "I guess you think we're a couple of crazies, don't you?"

"I sure as hell do," the bartender says. "Hell, man, you two throw away the stems. And that's the very best part."

* * * *

A hunter with an Irish setter and an English pointer walked into a tavern. They walk up to the bar and the guy says to the bartender, "If I can get my Irish setter to tell a few jokes for the folks in here, would you give me a couple of free drinks?"

The bartenders nods and the guy puts the setter in the middle of the floor and tells him to get started. Well, let me tell you, that setter is a sensation! The crowd has a ball! The bartender is ecstatic, saying, "Fantastic! Plumb wonderful. What a dog!"

And the owner says, "Hell, man, you ain't heard nothin' yet. My pointer is the ventriloquist that's doin' it all the talkin'!"

* * * *

Wicked: Extraordinarily good...or bad, as, "How was hunting?" "*Wicked. Plumb wicked.*"

* * * *

Did you hear about the two fellers who were a leetle shy of brains, maybe half a peck short of a bushel? Well, they went ice fishing. They were lucky and caught a whopper. But they came to a sad end...they drowned while frying it."

Here's another American myth — like those of Paul Bunyan, Pecos Bill, Johnny Appleseed. Meet Old Long John as good as the best of our heroes.

OLD LONG JOHN AND THE BEAR
by "Sulphur Fork," Bayou Chicot, Louisiana

This story appeared in **the Spirit**, XIX, No. 48 (January 19, 1850), 566; reprinted from the **New Orleans Delta**.

Old Long John, the Bear Hunter (as he always called himself), almost everyone west of the Mississippi is familiar with the name, that has almost as wide fame as the name of Daniel Boone. So long as the creeks and rivers continue to run through his old hunting grounds — Boggy Gutt, Beaver Creek, Turkey, Darbone, Calcasieu, and their tributaries — so long will his fame last.

On the first named is where he first settled after he came to this country in the year 1810. Being a great place for game at the time, it was the only inducement for his settling there, except that he also had a fine range of cattle and hogs. I have often heard him say that he never would have left old Carolina but for the want of a range for stock and the scarcity of game.

He was a man six feet four inches in height, weighed one hundred and eighty-five pounds, and was as erect as an Indian. His eye was more like an eagle's than any man's I ever saw. He died in his eighty-fifth year, about fifteen years ago. One month before his death he could stand on a level plane and jump thirty feet in three jumps. This will give some faint idea of what kind of specimen he was of the human species. In fact, I think he was the finest looking man I ever saw of his age.

I have often sat up with him in his pine log cabin of long winter nights by a cheerful pine-knot fire and heard him relate some of the most thrilling accounts of himself, and others, too, in the old Revolutionary War; and about hunting wild hogs, and bear and panther fights — some of which I know I never can forget, and one of which I will relate as he told it to me, word for word as near as I can remember.

Old Long John, the Bear Hunter, said: "One mornin' in May in the year 1810 — least ways it was blackberry time — I took Old Death in the Path (the name of his rifle) on my shoulder and belted Old Butcher around my waist, and off I started to look for a deer up Boggy Gutt. After I walked two or three miles and seein no deer, I begin to look for sign of other varmints. Now mind you — be G-- sirs, this is the truth I am tellin, and I want you all to listen. I know (said he) that it is a matter of long ago given up that all old hunters will lie, and I must acknowledge that I will lie a little, too, if you corner me too close about a bar fight — that is, if I have to shoot more than one time at it. It always discomboborates me to fight a bar in a canebrake with an empty gun, onless my dogs is might good — then I don't kere a fig; I jist walk right into 'em with Old Butcher (his knife). But if the dogs ain't true I always git mad, and then I am jist as apt to go right off from it as any other way.

And, as I was sayin, I was lookin for sign, and sure enough, be G-- sirs, I soon found plenty, right fresh and soft bar sign. I followed it up twill it come to a big bottle-ended holler stump of a tree that had been broke off about fifteen foot above the ground. I examined it well; I saw scratches and nail marks plenty on the stump; so I lent Old Death agin the tree and laid Old Butcher down by her. I thot I hearn something nestling inside the stump; so I tuck off my shoes and up it I went. When I come to the top, I looked in, I did, and what do you think I seed? Why two cub bar, be G-- sirs, rolling and playing down thar jist like two little kids.

Well, says I you're jist the critters I have been wanting for a long time for pets for the children. So I jist lumbered right down among them, I did. Then if you could a bin thar to hearn the fuss they kept up — sich hollerin and screaming! Oh! it beat any baby crying I ever hear, all holler. I got mad at last and begin to slap first one then tother to try to make um hush, but instead of that it made um ten times wors. I luckily kept my belt on; I let it out a few holes bigger and slipped one under it on each side, I did.

"Then, for the first time, I seed my sitivation. Now the holler of the stump was heep bigger at the bottom nor it was at the top, and I could get no foothold to climb out by. Man! I tell you, I was getin to feel mad then! — and them critters keeping sich a fuss, I could hear nothing else while they kept squalling. I jist sot down, I did, and studied, and studied, and studied what on yearth I should do to get outen this holler stump. Why you might jist as well try to climb out of a forty foot well that warn'rt curbed. I begin to think maybe the Old She might come along arter a while to suckel her young. Then I thought to myself, says I, I am in a nice fix here, a mile from home, in a holler tree, and no gun nor knife, and every prospect of a fight with an Old She, be G-- sirs! Man! I tell you, I was mad then!

All at once, while I was a-studyin about it, I heard the allfiredist rippet outside you ever heard; the Old She had come sure enough. Oh! I was mad then, I was. All at once, a thought struck me. I knowed that an Old She or a bar of any kind, indeed, could not bear to be fingered behind much, so I intended to act accordin. When she entered the top of the stump, she made all look dark below, I tell you, she did!

I got on my feet and waited twell I could jist cleverly reach her, I did — you know they always come down tail foremost. As soon as I could reach her, I grabbed her behind with both hands, and I give her the whoop, I did. If ever you saw a skeered bar — and I was mad, be G--, sirs — she took me faster than any railroad car twell she landed me about ten foot from the root of the stump, flat on my belly, she did. Oh man! I was mad! but sort a stuntified like by the fall. Before I could get Old Death, she was clean outen sight, and a-running."

* * * *

Charley met a bear,
The bear met Charley.
The bear was bulgy,
The bulge was Charley.

Used up: Worn out, as, "After trampin' them fields all day I was some *used up*."

* * * *

Game warden: "You're under arrest, mister. Rabbits are out of season!"

Hunter: "Out of season, hell! I had no choice because this dadblamed rabbit was vicious! He attacked me! Warden, I had to kill the bloodthirsty critter in self-defense!"

* * * *

She: "I admire you so very much."

He: "Why?"

She: "Didn't you tell me that you hunt bear?"

He: "Nope! You got it wrong. I hunt fully clothed!"

* * * *

Gunmen's sidewalk: Since all hunters are not in search of birds and beasts, but some hunt for men, the *gunmen's sidewalk* is an old western phrase meaning the middle of the street, a good place from which to see all sides and avoid ambush.

* * * *

"How's the state of yore mind an' the stem of yore constitution?": A nice and friendly way of inquiring after a fellow hunter's well-being. Much friendlier than, "How are ya?"

* * * *

Eddie Jones decided to try winter hunting in northern Montana. Accordingly, he arranged to rent a cabin on Fort Peck Lake. But when he got there, it was cold...snappin' cold! The only windbreak between the cabin and the North Pole was a barbed wire fence, and two strands were missing!

Eddie had plenty of good grub with him, but no meat. So he stowed his gear in the cabin, lit a fire, and went hunting. He'd hardly got out the door when a

Canada goose came wingin' past and he ups, leads and fires. But not a sound came from the gun...the sound had frozen before Eddie could hear it! Yep, and the buckshot froze, too. The wind blew it back at him, but he ducked just in time and only a few buckshot nicked him, and he picked them out of his hide later on.

By this time, Eddie was cold. So, he went inside to the fire he'd built earlier. But the fire now gave no heat. It had frozen in the fireplace! Well, nothing to do but break it in pieces and carry the flames outside and dump them. By this time, Eddie was pretty discouraged and cold and tired. So he hit the sack.

Early the next morning, he was awakened by a loud "bang!" He rushed outside to see what had happened. A blast of warm air hit him. Temperature had moderated during the night and had thawed the shotgun blast which had detonated (tardily) now that the air was unfrozen.

But that wasn't all. Right before his eyes, those frozen flames came completely unfrozen, blazed up and caught the grass on fire. Luckily, there was a fire extinguisher in the cabin, and he managed to put out the grassfire.

Eddie packed up and went home. So far as we know, he has since then confined his hunting and fishing to his home state of Missouri.

* * * *

Once a hunter gets himself married, he knows he's really and truly hitched when his wife barks at him and his dog...brings his slippers.

* * * *

Rammin': Out on a spree...on the town, as, "Old Al couldn't come huntin' with us today. He was out *rammin'* last night and overdone it."

TELLING LIES

After I'd been out shooting chukar partridge with Larry Dinovitz, the head man of the Rocking K Ranch in Bishop, California, we got together over what the cowboys used to call "tongue oil." And as things got along in conversation, Larry got to telling lies about his Labrador, Charlie. And I got to telling lies about my Labradors, Tippy and Judy. Larry, being a gentleman at heart, started out easy with half-mile retrieves and I countered with three-quarter mile retrieves — on doubles. Then Larry mentioned that Charlie's work on these half-mile retrieves was on giant Canada geese and I added that my three-quarter milers were through a couple of inches of ice. Well, Larry's dog got going nearer and nearer to Alaska and mine got to plowing through stuff that the Coast Guard icebreaker Eastwind would flinch at and we started to call it a draw. Larry mixed another batch and suddenly Charlie rose up from under Larry's feet behind the bar and started to bark. Larry said, with a straight face, that Charlie was pretty good at mixing drinks and was reminding him that he had forgotten to add the Triple Sec to the Margueritas. I didn't say anything, Larry being the host, but I really don't believe that any Labrador retriever can tell the difference between Triple Sec and Cointreau. Even mine.

— Gene Hill. Outdoor Yarns and Outright Lies.
Stackpole Books 1983. Harrisburg, PA.

✳ ✳ ✳ ✳

THE ANSWER MAN SHOOTS GOLF

Dear Answer Man,

I have been invited by my boss to go "golf shooting" with him and some important clients. Not wishing to appear ignorant, I'd like a little information about this sport before I go. Frankly, I haven't heard of golfs at all and I'm in the dark. Please fill me in.

Chester

Dear Chester,

Aha! Golfs! I have a little experience with these creatures, and feel happy that you came to the Source for your help.

My experience with shooting golfs happened several years ago when two gentlemen (I'll call them Joe and Frank) asked me if I would like to try this version of organized lunacy. Not having the Source to guide me (as you are so fortunate to have, all false modesty aside), I agreed with some trepidation.

These two picked me up and we headed for the golfs shooting grounds. Now, right off, I was turned off. They brought no dogs and walk-up shooting without dogs ranks, for me, right next to a root canal on the pleasure scale. In any event, I agreed that perhaps there was something here to learn.

Arriving at the shooting grounds, I found that Frank and Joe harbored sadistic streaks heretofore cleverly concealed — they were going to do their hunting with what they called "golf clubs." Naturally, I had visions of the Canadian harp seal hunt, squabbles with Greenpeace, and maybe your odd restraining order from a bleeding-heart-commie-pinko federal judge. But, I persevered.

I noticed rather quickly that golfs had an overpopulation problem. They had evidently grazed the grass down to where it wouldn't have kept together the body and soul of an undersized goat. There appeared to be no winter-over cover, just a few trees here and there with virtually no understory of shrubs to foil any avian predators.

I also noticed that there seemed to be a large number of other hunters, dressed in loud colors to avoid being clubbed, I assumed. The sweaters they wore all had little alligators on the breast, and I took this as some sort of initiation badge denoting bravery.

We checked in at the clubhouse and paid our shooting fee. Frank looked at me funny when I asked how many golfs were released for our party for the 10 bucks I just plunked down.

Moving out onto the shooting grounds, I watched as my two cohorts changed into spiked shoes, which naturally made me nervous. I mean, I hate hunting game that has to be stomped on to finally reduce to possession. I was given some of the clubs, and when I asked about their use, Joe told me something about distance, which I translated into meaning that the club with a "9" on it was like improved cylinder and the big club (an antique — still made of wood) with the "1" on it was like full choke. After that, I got a little fuzzy.

It soon became apparent that you searched for golfs by looking in their holes. Evidently, the creatures stay in colonies of exactly 18 such habitats, and hunting them consists of walking from spot to spot and looking in the holes. I wondered how we could have any luck doing this because it seemed to me that the hunters just before us were doing the same thing and having no luck.

And here, I must add an amusing footnote: golf hunting is so unproductive, that the hunters amuse themselves by knocking a little white ball around (which I mistook for a golf egg) from hole to hole. This apparently is the golf hunter's equivalent of the gin rummy game that keeps goose hunters occupied between fights. I figured as long as you have to walk from hole to hole, that hitting the little ball with the club was as good a way as any to keep my sanity.

In fact, I once hit my little ball toward the next golf hole (marked with a flag — can you believe it, talk about a tame preserve) and the darn thing went into the golf hole on the first hit. Frank and Joe looked shocked, and I was mad — I had to walk all the way to the hole with nothing to do except watch those two jerks!

Anyhow, Frank kept writing on a little card, evidently a way that he cooperates with the game department about how many golfs we sighted (or didn't). But, the sonuvagun lied. He said that, at the end, he had seen 84 golfs, Joe had seen 90, and I had seen 141 golfs! Whattacrock! I never saw one! And, since he claimed I had the highest total, I had to buy the mash 'n splash!

So, golf hunters have to be put in the same category as trap shooters, snipe hunters, and other similar, emotionally unstable folks — not to be trusted.

So, Chester, I wish you luck. If you shoot any golfs, send me a picture of one, fercryinoutloud.

— Gene Hill & Steve Smith. Outdoor Yarns And Outright Lies.
Stackpoles Books 1983. Harrisburg, PA.

✻ ✻ ✻ ✻

Here are two hilarious stories by that accomplished, unique writer on hunting and fishing, Charley Dickey. FIELD & STREAM, OUTDOOR LIFE, PETERSON'S HUNTING and many others have been graced by this man's superb, humorous tales.

REAL MEN DON'T WEAR PANTYHOSE

I knew I was getting into trouble when Herman talked me into buying those pantyhose!

There are convenient ways of getting in shape for most hunting trips — climbing steps for grouse hunts or doing arm exercises before paddling a canoe to moose bogs. But there's no way you can get your bottom ready for a pack trip on horseback except by riding a horse.

From my city apartment it's not easy to reach a stable that rents horses, especially at a rate I can afford. One year, before a pack trip for muleys in Wyoming, I rode a bicycle for weeks but it didn't help. Another year I spent a lot of time straddling a motor bike and sliding down bannisters. It didn't get me ready for the saddle torture waiting in Idaho.

You'd think an office job, where you're on and off a chair all day, would prepare your seat for riding a horse. Not one bit. One season I took a sawhorse to the office, put a saddle on it and used it for a desk chair. It might have worked, but secretaries from all over the building kept sneaking in for a look. They'd giggle, rush out the door to get their friends, and you could hear them laughing all the way to the elevator. The boss suggested I remove the contraption, immediately!

If, straight from the city, you've never ridden a pack horse for ten hours, you don't know what pure misery is.

It's worse than being sacked all afternoon by the Minnesota Vikings. The next morning you can survive the aches and cramps, but what kills you are the great red patches of chafed skin. It's easier to walk bowlegged all day than to face the mere thought of climbing back on your horse. Even a four-gaited horse doesn't have any easy riding gear if your loins and bottom are chafed raw. Talk about pouring turpentine on an open wound, man, you can't touch your sensitive acreage of chafes with a powderpuff!

The chafing stays with you the whole trip, getting more tender each day. Your muscles break loose every morning about the time the sun comes over the peaks. But if you have a chafing garden, it's just grind, grind, grind all day. It gets to burning so bad you can't think of anything but salves and lotions. If the crew wouldn't get disgusted, you'd be glad to return to camp and hunt jays and magpies, lying flat on your back, or course.

It was my city luncheon friend, Herman, who told me how to prevent chafing. All I had to do was wear a pair of pantyhose. According to Herman the thin layer of nylon slides and prevents friction on vital parts. There's no heating and chafing. Herman is the one who spends his winter weekends in New England hunting for Abominable Snowmen and the summer searching for the Loch Ness monster in Central Park. Herman says he's seen both, many times.

I was planning a trip to Montana's high country and ready to try anything. The more I thought about pantyhose preventing chafing, the better the idea sounded. There was just one catch! Suppose the pack crew saw me putting them on some morning? Or taking them off? I'd be the butt of every trail joke from Yuma to Kalispell. I could hear the wranglers in the bars laughing about the dude who wore pantyhose. By the time the story was told three times, they'd have me wearing a brassiere.

Herman said that was no problem — simply never let the wranglers see me dressing or going to the bathroom in the bushes. Nothing to it.

When I arrived in Whitefish and met the crew, I tried to think of some way to get rid of the three pairs of pantyhose in my duffel. The guide looked like one of the heavies who almost whips Matt Dillon, the wrangler obviously belonged to the Key Hole gang, and the one-eyed Indian cook with the scarred face wore a scalping knife on his belt.

I lay awake all night in the bunkhouse. I desperately wanted to wear those pantyhose but the thought of being caught in them made me cringe. The convincer was the horrible memory of past suffering.

Before anyone stirred, I slipped from my bunk, eased a pair of pantyhose from the cellophane package, and quickly put them on, frantically looking around to see if anyone was watching. After I got them covered with my britches, I was pleasantly surprised how comfortable they felt. Then I woke the others and went outside to check the weather.

We had a good start toward the Continental Divide before the first rest stop. I eased away from the others. My legs and bottom felt great! There was no irritation and outside of a few twinging calf muscles, I felt like I'd been riding on a fluffy pillow. The crew and I warmed up to each other and we joked about the great elk I'd shoot to break the Boone and Crockett record.

You might think it's easy to go to the bathroom away from everyone in the vast wilderness of the big sky country. Just try it! While there's always a certain modesty on the trail, I knew the others were thinking I was unusually shy. Whenever I stood up to leave the campfire, everything seemed to get deathly silent. If I made an excuse to leave the guide, I thought he looked at me rather strangely.

I got a bad run in the first pair of pantyhose and couldn't think of any way to get rid of them. After everyone was asleep, I crawled out of camp and buried the hose like a thief in the night.

The crew must have thought I was the most eager dude they'd ever had. I was always up before anyone else and the last to hit his bedroll. I was careful to keep the spare pantyhose hidden and kept checking my gear. Then I got to worrying that would make them think I was checking to see if they had stolen something.

I worried that I might oversleep and have to get up and dress in front of them and my dreadful secret would be out. Then I got to wondering what would happen if I broke a leg and when they put the splint on they discovered the pantyhose. What if a bear broke into camp and scattered everything and they saw my spare pantyhose? I even crawled out one night to see if anything had dug up that pair I'd buried.

It was the best trail crew I'd ever hunted with but I just knew they were whispering about me. I considered making a clean breast of the whole thing. Around the fire some evening, when everyone was jovial, I'd yank my britches down and holler, "Want to see something funny?"

I thought of confiding in the guide but decided he couldn't keep from laughing. If I tried it with the wrangler, I knew he'd go into hysteria. I considered telling the Indian, saying pantyhose were a spiritual charm in my family. Perhaps he might understand. On the other hand, he might hurt himself rolling on the ground.

I worked myself into a real tizzy and was glad to shoot an elk on the ninth day so we could get out of there. It wasn't a record rack but we were all happy with it. That night, I crawled out and buried the remaining pantyhose, figuring I could get back down the mountain without chafing. I relaxed considerably and was singing as we got to the ranch. I told everybody we'd go to town and the drinks were on me.

They were all for it as soon as they put their horses up and sorted out their gear. I followed them over to the laundry room and watched them put their duds in the electric washer. The guide put in three pairs of pantyhose, the wrangler put in three, and the Indian added four.

TRAINING THE OUTDOOR WIFE

Training a wife is one of the most difficult jobs an outdoorsman faces.

One reason is that he doesn't acquire her during her early formative years. By the time he meets her, she may have undesirable habit patterns so firmly ingrained that it takes great patience to teach her the correct way to do things.

The best time to start training a puppy is when it's seven weeks old. It's easy then, but if you wait until the dog is two or three years old, you can sponsor a stomach ulcer just trying to change some small detail.

A lot of wives are not biddable. Perhaps, there are some who could not have been trained properly even if their educations had started at a tender age.

When a hunter goes on an afternoon trip, his estimated time of arrival back home is probably correct within plus or minus three hours. A few hunters may need the ETA leeway increased to a week on the long side but this is far from being the norm.

One of Charley's Principles states that if a fisherman has promised to be home at 7 P.M., the fish will start hitting at the exact moment he has to leave in order to make his designated arrival time.

The same principle applies to hunting. If company is coming for an early supper, just as the hunter is starting to leave the woods he will see the biggest buck of his life. Further, the buck will disappear in an island of cover the hunter is sure he can quickly work. A lot of hunters learn to live on midnight snacks during the deer season.

It's the time factor which women can't get the hang of. They don't understand that hunting and fishing are for relaxation, and if you're on a rigid time schedule, there's no relaxation. Some wives are unreasonable about punctuality, which is what you have to do when you go to work.

For instance, a friend of mine found a deer scrape at noon. It was the first fresh one he had found all season, and he was the only hunter around. Naturally, he took a stand to wait for the buck to return, and it is totally understandable that he forgot he was to be married at 4 P.M.

When he arrived at the church at six, the bride was considerably perturbed. He explained over and over that just because you locate a fresh scrape doesn't mean the buck will show up right away. Sometimes you have to keep going back for two or three days!

He tried to calm her down by explaining that the buck had eight points. He had the buck in his car to prove it! He wanted to take her whole family out to the parking lot to see the rack but nobody seemed interested. No matter how many times he explained the logic of why he was late, she couldn't seem to grasp the point.

Anyway, the ceremony was held after they went by his apartment so he could get out of his hunting clothes and into a suit. The consensus among their friends was that the groom might have been trying to push the bride's education a little too fast.

When I leave home for an afternoon hunt, my wife always wants to know what to do about supper. Well, the last thing I'm concerned with is eating. I have enough on my mind trying to find my boots and making major decisions like what rifle to take.

In reply, I have a little song I usually sing to the tune of "I'll Be Down to Get You in a Taxi, Honey." It goes, "Leave my supper in the oven, honey. I sure do go for a half-burnt steak." I really shouldn't sing that song because it seems to infuriate her. Of course, she knew before we were married that I wasn't much of a singer.

Wives seem to think that going hunting or fishing is like going to the movies. The show starts at a certain time, and all you have to do is be there a few minutes early and you know what time you'll get out.

On a hunt last fall, I promised to be back at 7 P.M., since my wife's mother was arriving for a visit. I would have made it on time except just as I started to leave at dusk I got a shot at a four-pointer.

I'm not very handy at dressing a deer in broad daylight. I always hope that another hunter will volunteer to do it to gain woodsman experience. But I was by myself and did the best I could in the dark.

In all honesty, I did arrive home in a crimson condition. When I drove into the garage, my wife and mother-in-law came out to greet me. My mother-in-law took one look, shrieked, and ran back into the house screaming, "I always told you he'd come to a bad end!"

I knew that my wife was trying to be patient and understanding. You can always tell by the way she grinds her teeth.

"Well," she shouted, "you knew my mother was coming, and the least you could have done was shoot that deer by three o'clock."

Like I said, women just can't get the hang of this time thing. It seems like educating a wife is a life-time project.

OPENING SHOTS AND PARTING LINES,
Charley Dickey. Winchester Press, 1983.

✳ ✳ ✳ ✳

THE PARTRIDGE AND THE SWEATER

Did you ever hear how Mardi Bass right here shot the partridge? Well, last fall Mardi was coming along that same road from Seboomook to Caucomgomoc when she spied a partridge and took a shot at him. She didn't kill him, but she knocked all the feathers off him. When Mardi got home she felt so badly about it she sat right down and knitted that partridge a sweater, and put it on him, and let him go. This spring Mardi saw that partridge with five little partridges behind, all wearing little sweaters. And one of them had the prettiest little feather-necked ruff you ever saw.

HOW TO TAN A SQUIRREL SKIN

The last time I drove through the upper Adirondacks I stopped in to see Uncle John Eichelberger, the Hermit of Bog Lake. He was celebrating his eighty-second birthday by bucksawing a cord of hardwood, but he knocked off when I came up the trail, and we had a drink of Charley Coomey's applejack to his health. It is Uncle John's considered opinion that anyone who would fritter away his time fishing would suck eggs, and when the subject came up (as it always does), I ventured to remark that I knew some fairly intelligent people who fished. Uncle John snorted so loud that his pet chipmunk jumped two feet in the air.

"Bushwah!" yelled Uncle John. "Lemme tell you, young feller, I seen a heap of fishermen in my time, and there wasn't one of em could hold a candle to a bluejay fer makin' sense. Used to be a preacher name of Henry Van Something-or-other come by here ever' so often. Folks said he wrote books and was right clever, and I vow he didn't have sense enough to come in out the rain. Leastwise he always carried a raincoat whilst fishin'. What'd you do with that jug, now? Thankee. Now like I wuz sayin'. I remember one time when I wuz jest a whippersnapper, my daddy sent me out to git him a gray squirrel. 'And take care you don't shoot it in the head,' he says, 'fer I want the brains of it to tan the skin with.' So I went squirrelin', but the only one I see jest had his head sticken' out a crotch, so I shot him anyway. When I got home my daddy was fit to be tied on account of not havin' the critter's brains to cure the skin with. Then he remembered there wuz a party of three fishermen from the city that wuz campin' down by the beaver darn, and give me the gun and told me to shoot one of them fishermen. Hand me that jug, bub."

"What are you trying to prove?" I asked, while Uncle John refilled his glass.

"Nothin'," Uncle John said, tossing off the tumbler of apple. "Only except I had to shoot all three of them fishermen to get enough brains to tan a squirrel skin."

ACKNOWLEDGEMENTS

We are indebted to Laurie Bartolini, Pat Blinn, Mike Dicus, Marie Ellen Halcli, Jenny Holmberg, Classie Murray, Chris Wagner and Julie Wullner of the Reference Department and Janna Mohan and Jean Ann Long of the Interlibrary Loan Department of the Lincoln Library, Springfield, Illinois; and Vicky Zemaitis, Reference Department and Sondra Hastings, Interlibrary Loan Department, Illinois State Library, Springfield, Illinois.

BIBLIOGRAPHY

Absolutely Mad Inventions. Dover Publications, Inc. 1960.

American Legion Magazine. Reprinted by permission, The American Legion Magazine, © 1951 and 1953.

America's Golly Whoppers & Tall Tales. The Best of the Burlington Liar's Club, © 1981 by Robert Deindorfer. Reprinted by permission of Workman Publishing Company. All rights reserved.

Are Fishermen People? Ed Zern. Harper & Brothers, New Jersey. 1955.

Argosy Magazine. Material from Argosy Magazine reprinted by permission of Argosy Communications, Inc. Copyright © 1990 Argosy Communications, Inc. All rights reserved.

Buffalo Fish at Fish Market. Gruss Collection, 1001.0012. Missouri Historical Society. St. Louis, MO.

Burlington Liar's Club. John Soeth, President. Burlington, WI. Calling All Fly-Fishers. Alan D'Egville. Curtis Brown. London. 1949.

Cartoons by Dave Carpenter. Emmetsburg, IA

Cartoons by Dan Earlywine. Chatham, IL

Cartoons by James Estes. Amarillo, TX

Cartoons by Lo Linkert. Port Coquitlam, B.C.

Cartoon by Cavilli. Reprinted with permission from The Saturday Evening Post.

Cartoon by Lepper. Reprinted with permission from The Saturday Evening Post.

Catfish At The Pump. Roger L. Welsch with Linda K. Welsch. University of Nebraska Press. Lincoln, NE. 1982.

Curing The Cross-Eyed Mule. Loyal Jones and Billy Edd Wheeler. August House Publishers. Little Rock, AR. 1989.

Don't Blame The Fish. Bob Warner. Winchester Press. New York. 1974.

Fish And Be Damned. Lawrence Lariar. Used by permission of the publisher, Prentice-Hall, Inc., Englewood Cliffs, N.J. 1953. 1981.

Fishin' For Fun — And To Wash Your Soul. Herbert Hoover. Random House. New York. 1963.

Fishin' Fun — A Treasury of Fishing Humor. W.A. Brooks. Derby Press, Inc. 1954.

Fishing: An Angler's Dictionary. Henry Beard and Roy McKie. Reprinted by permission of Workman Publishing Company. All rights reserved. Copyright 1983.

Fish Story. From BENNETT CERF'S TREASURY OF ATROCIOUS PUNS. Copyright © 1968 by Phyllis Cerf Wagener, Christopher B. Cerf and Jonathan F. Cerf. Reprinted by permission of Harper & Row, Publishers, Inc. Funny Stories From Arkansas. Vance Randolph. Haldeman-Julius. Girard, KS. 1949.

Game Warden? Shoot the S.O.B. Volumes I and II. Harold Hoey. Marshall, MO.

Handy As Hip Pickets On A Hog. Donald Chain Black. The Taylor Publishing Company. Dallas, TX.

Hit, Haint The Fish (The Great Tennessee Fox Hunt). Nat T. Winston. Southern Publishers. Kingsport, TN. 1949.

Hot Springs And Hell. Vance Randolph. Folklore
Association. Hatboro, PA. 1965.

How To Catch Fishermen. Ed Zern. Appleton-Century-Croft,
Inc. New York. 1951.

How To Fish Good. Milford ("Stanley") Poltroon. Winchester
Press. New York. 1971.

Hunters, Fishermen And Other Liars. Lo Linkert. Plainsman
Publications. Vancouver, British Columbia. 1979.

Illinois State Journal. Column by Toby McDaniels.
Springfield, IL

Joe Creason's Kentucky. Joe Creason. The Louisville
Courier. 1972. Reprinted by permission of Bill Creason.

Jokelore. Ronald L. Baker. Indiana University Press.
Bloomington, IN. 1986.

Laughter In Appalachia. Loyal Jones and Billy Edd Wheeler.
August House Publishers. Little Rock, AR. 1987.

Mark Twain In Eruption. Ed. by Bernard DeVoto. Harper &
Bros. New York. 1922.

Nothin' Ain't No Good. E.P. Holmes. Clay Printing Co. 1955.
Now I'll Tell One. O.C. Hulett. The Reilly & Lee Co.,
Publishers. Chicago, IL. 1935.

Ol' Hunters Never Lie. Bill Wilson. Ashcraft Printers, Inc.
Kansas City, MO. 1985.

Opening Shots and Parting Lines. Charley Dickey. "Real
Men Don't Wear Pantyhose" Petersen's Hunting. April 1974.
"Training the Outdoor Wife" Georgia Sportsman. October
1978.

Outdoor Yarns and Outright Lies. Gene Hill and Steve Smith.
Stackpole Books. Harrisburg, PA. 1983.

Ozark Mountain Humor. W.K. McNeil, Editor. August House,
Inc., Publishers. Little Rock, AR. 1989.

Pye-Eyed Pete's Unnatural History. Dave Stirling. 1943.
Reprinted by permission of Dave Schutz. Estes Park, CO.

Shingling The Fog and Other Plains Lies. Roger L. Welsch. University of Nebraska Press. Lincoln, NE. 1972.

"Song to Catfish" from SOUPSONGS by Roy Blount, Jr. Copyright © 1987 by Roy Blount, Jr. Reprinted by permission of Houghton Mifflin Company.

Stories of the Old Duck Hunters and Other Drivel. Gordon MacQuarrie. Stackpole Books. Harrisburg, PA. 1967.

Tall Tales Are Not All From Texas. Bill Ring. Reprinted by permission of Ring & Associates. Melbourne, FL.

Texas Brags. John Randolph. Texas. 1945.

The Fish In My Life. Murray Hoyt. Crown Publishers, Inc. New York. 1964.

This Fishy Business — From Noah's Ark to Billingsgate. S. John Peskett. Thorton Buttersworth Ltd. London. 1935.

To Hell With Fishing. Ed Zern & H.P. Webster. D. Appleton-Century Co., New York. 1945.

To Hell With Hunting. Ed Zern. D. Appleton-Century Co., Inc. New York. 1946.

Upstream, Downstream and Out of My Mind. Syd Hoff. Bobbs Merrill. Indianapolis, IN. 1961.

Walt Mason — His Book. Walt Mason. Barse & Hopkins. New York. 1911.

We Always Lie to Strangers. Vance Randolph. Columbia University Press. New York. 1951.

We have made every effort to contact the original sources used herein and hope we have not inadvertently overlooked any of them. If we have, we apologize and request that they contact the publisher.

Here is a list of the current books of superb humor published by the Lincoln-Herndon Press, Inc.

The humor in these books will delight you, brighten your conversation, make your life more fun, and healthier, because "Laughter Is The Best Medicine."

*Grandpa's Rib-Ticklers & Knee-Slappers	$8.95
*Josh Billings —	
America's Phunniest Phellow	$7.95
Davy Crockett —	
Legendary Frontier Hero	$7.95
Cowboy Life on the Sidetrack	$7.95
A Treasury of Science Jokes	$8.95
The Great American Liar — Tall Tales	$9.95
The Cowboy Humor of A.H. Lewis	$9.95
The Fat Mascot...	
22 Funny Baseball Stories & More	$7.95
A Treasury of Farm & Ranch Humor	$10.95
Mr. Dooley...We Need Him Now!	
The Irish-American Humorist	$8.95
A Treasury of Military Humor	$10.95
Here's Charley Weaver, Mamma and Mt. Idy	$9.95
A Treasury of Hunting and Fishing Humor	$10.95

*These books are also available in hardback.

Order From:

Lincoln-Herndon Press, Inc.
818 South Dirksen Parkway
Springfield, Illinois 62703